Paul Newman
and
Joanne Woodward

Paul Newman
and
Joanne Woodward

Susan Netter

PIATKUS

Copyright © 1989 by Ultra Communications Inc.

This edition first published in
Great Britain in 1989 by
Judy Piatkus (Publishers) Ltd of
5 Windmill Street, London W1

British Library Cataloguing in Publication Data

Netter, Susan
  Paul Newman and Joanne Woodward: a biography, *Susan, Netter*
  1. Cinema films. Acting. Newman, Paul 1925 – .
  Woodward, Joanne. Newman, Paul, 1925 – & Woodward, Joanne
  I. Title
  791.43′028′0922

  ISBN 0 86188 869 3

Phototypeset in 11/13pt Compugraphic Plantin by
Action Typesetting, Gloucester
Printed and bound in Great Britain by
Butler & Tanner Ltd, Frome, Somerset

To my Aunt Dorris and Uncle Dick,
another world-class couple.

Acknowledgements

The Publishers would like to thank Pictorial Parade and Frank Edwards Fotos International for permission to use the photographs.

Introduction

Paul Newman and Joanne Woodward. Together and separately they have become legends in their own time, admired, respected and loved by millions of fans the world over. As far as landmark films and *tour de force* performances go, this pair has contributed an incredible legacy to cinematic history.

Yet, the story of the private life shared by Paul and Joanne is just as fascinating. Deeply dedicated to charitable causes, the Newmans have chosen a quiet and unusual existence in Westport, Connecticut, far away from the glamour and glitz of Hollywood. They have raised three children of their own, as well as helped rear Paul's kids by his first marriage. And, amazingly enough by show biz standards, they recently celebrated their 30th wedding anniversary.

Paul and Joanne first met when she was 22 and he was 27 in the original Broadway production of *Picnic,* William Inge's play. Newman was in the leading male role, while Joanne, then an aspiring young actress from Georgia, was understudying both Janice Rule's and Kim Stanley's parts. Paul and Joanne made friends immediately, but because Paul was already married (to Jacqueline White) and a father, they tried to remain simply friends, fighting the passionate attraction they both felt.

After *Picnic* Joanne Woodward burst onto the movie screen like a meteor, winning the Academy Award for best actress at the tender age of 28 for her haunting portrayal of a schizophrenic woman in *The Three Faces of Eve*. After enjoying a modicum of success in *Somebody Up There Likes Me* for his depiction of Rocky Graziano, Newman was paired with his old friend, longtime love and soon-to-be wife Joanne Woodward in *The Long, Hot Summer*. On-screen the duo sizzled, and marriage followed in 1958.

It was a different time then, and in spite of being an Oscar winner, young wife Joanne Woodward vowed, 'I will not let a career separate me from Paul.' Her career went on hold, as she, along with their infant daughter, Nell, accompanied Paul to Israel on location for *Exodus*. During the first decade of their marriage, nearly all the films Joanne made were with her husband.

For many years, Paul was grist for the Hollywood starmaker mill. He made many excellent films, in which he created unforgettable characters on screen, but for years no one took Paul Newman seriously as an actor. The reason? He was too good-looking. As George Roy Hill, who directed Newman in *The Sting*, put it: 'He makes it look so easy, and he looks so wonderful, that everybody assumes he isn't acting.' It was a case of the public thinking a star couldn't be both beefcake material and a tour de force actor at the same time.

Paul was cast in a series of roles as alienated rebels and anti-heroes of various sorts. He was a pool shark in *The Hustler*, a gigolo in *Sweet Bird of Youth*, a tough guy in both *Hud* and *Cool Hand Luke*, an outlaw in *Butch Cassidy and the Sundance Kid*, a charming con artist in *The Sting*.

By then it was 1973, and for the rest of that decade Paul, discouraged by the poor roles offered to him, concentrated more on car racing than acting. He even considered quitting films for good.

Instead, as the 1980s dawned, Paul Newman's career took an upswing. At the age of 56, he was suddenly in demand for 'meaty' character roles. In rapid succession, he made *Fort*

Apache, The Bronx, Absence of Malice, and *The Verdict.* The latter film, in which Paul portrayed a has-been alcoholic lawyer trying to make a comeback in court, won high critical praise, and many felt that Paul, nominated five times, should have won the best actor Oscar for it. Instead he was awarded a Life Achievement Award from the Academy, an accolade usually reserved for much older actors, virtually retired from films.

Then along came *The Color of Money,* a sequel to *The Hustler,* in which Paul played opposite Tom Cruise, recreating his role as Fast Eddie Felson, pool hustler. While this film was artistically inferior to the original *Hustler,* all the principal actors turned in excellent performances, especially Paul Newman. Finally, after some 47 films and six Oscar nominations, Paul won the best actor award in 1987 for his superb portrayal of a seasoned older Eddie, who plays mentor to protégé Cruise.

Meanwhile, Joanne Woodward, a gifted actress in her own right, was forced by the facts of life for women in Hollywood, and marriage, to slacken her own career pace. Deferring to her husband's greater stardom, she appeared in many of his films as a kind of female side-kick. Her own unique talent went underground as she bore three children, helped to bring up Paul's children from his first marriage, and devoted herself to humanitarian causes and artistic interests.

At the age of 35, Joanne slowly began to nurture her own creativity again. She began to take ballet classes – and developed a passionate love for the art, becoming a patron rather than a performer. She also optioned a Canadian novel called *A Jest of God,* helped develop it into a screenplay entitled *Rachel, Rachel,* and starred in it under her husband's direction, since no one else was interested in backing or directing it. It became a labour of love for both of them, a mutual artistic achivement, and a popular success.

Their respective film careers, however, are only part of Paul and Joanne's compelling story. Equally intriguing is the private life they have shared together for more than 30 years. Not only is their union remarkable for its duration, almost unheard of for a show biz couple, but also for its character. Paul and Joanne eschewed Hollywood-style living more than 20 years ago in favour of a quiet and decidely low-key life in Westport, Connecticut, a suburban New York enclave favoured by writers and artists. The couple live in a 200-year old farmhouse which has a real river running by it, an apple orchard, and eleven acres of woods and fields. There, amid dogs and cats and daughters, the Newmans have found privacy and peace – and plenty of time for each other.

They have also found the time to pursue their own separate careers and interests. Paul devotes the summer months to sports car racing, a hobby he has pursued avidly and successfully for some 15 years. He also keeps busy with his burgeoning food business, Newman's own brand of salad dressing, popcorn and spaghetti sauce. All of the company's considerable profits go to charity. Paul is also co-founder of a fully-funded camp for children with terminal illnesses. Both he and Joanne are political liberals who work for causes such as nuclear disarmament and civil rights.

Joanne, who enjoys opera, ballet, and highbrow culture of all kinds, has channelled her talents (both acting and directorial) into live theatre. 'Let's face it,' she says philosophically, 'Paul is the movie star. Films aren't offered to me like they once were.'

Besides performing in summer season plays, which she enjoys, and in various off-Broadway productions, Woodward has also starred in several TV movies. One of these, *The Shadow Box*, in whch Joanne portrayed a 'drunken sexpot,' was particularly savoured by Paul, who directed it. He later bragged to a reporter that his wife was 'a functioning voluptuary.'

But are the Newmans really happy? Can any celebrity marriage endure and satisfy both partners? Do Paul and Joanne still find each other interesting and sexy after more than 30 years? Are their careers still rewarding? Are their contributions of time and money to charities of all kinds, from the arts to famine victims in Africa, borne out of caring or radical chic?

The answers to these and other questions about one of America's most well known celebrity couples are here in this book, which for the first time fully chronicles the life of the pair everyone knows as Paul and Joanne.

Chapter 1

The snow was three feet deep and the temperature registered well below zero on January 26, 1925. Yet at least one child born that day, in Cleveland, Ohio, seemed the personification of summer, with his shock of blonde hair and his sky-blue eyes. The eight-pound boy was healthy, well-formed and handsome from day one. His parents named him Paul Leonard Newman.

Even though he was their second son, born merely a year after the first, Arthur S. Newman, Jr., this new addition to the Newman family was welcomed eagerly. Both parents were second generation Americans; Arthur Newman, Sr. of German-Jewish descent, and Theresa Fetzer of Hungarian-Catholic heritage. Because his family owned a very successful sporting goods store, Arthur Newman, Sr. was able to support his growing family in style. Paul and his older brother grew up in an 11-room house in Shaker Heights, one of Cleveland's choicest suburbs.

The family, which was highly respected and well-liked, did not flaunt its wealth, however. The Newmans eschewed the snobbish social cliques in favour of traditional, home values which stressed the importance of the family and hard work. The Newman boys were never spoiled. Despite their wealth, Arthur, Jr. and Paul were taught that rewards had to be earned and that one should avoid being wasteful or extravagant at all costs. It is said that while their neighbourhood playmates had deluxe baseball mitts (purchased at the Newman's very own sporting goods store) by the ages of six or seven, Arthur and Paul each had to wait until the age of ten to receive theirs.

The fact that Paul's two parents were of different religions did not seem to pose a problem in the Newman household. Paul's father passed on some of the tenets of Judaism in an informal way. As for his mother, Paul explained, 'She left the Catholic Church to become a Christian Scientist, and that's the way she raised me. But I don't practise that faith or anything like it today.' Paul often specifically cited his Jewish heritage, even in the early 1950s when many actors considered it wise to hide any Jewish background to avoid prejudice and not jeopardise audience appeal.

As a boy growing up, Paul Newman was said to be average in almost every way. His grades at school were good but not great, he had an easy-going, pleasant personality, and of course, his good looks. The only problem was his short stature – and perhaps his attempts to compensate for it. At any rate, Paul said that because of it, 'I used to get the bejesus kicked out of me regularly in school.'

Outside of school, he enjoyed the usual pursuits of suburban boyhood. He fished, played baseball, and climbed trees with the other kids in spring and summer. During the long winters, he enjoyed skating and tobogganing. Paul and his older brother, Arthur, had a close relationship, largely devoid of sibling rivalry. Rather than being overbearing, Arthur was protective toward his younger brother. To this day they remain close. Now a film production manager who lives in Lake Arrowhead, California, Arthur stays in close touch with Paul and the two have worked together on film projects.

Even though no cause and effect relationship can be established, there were two influences of a cultural and creative nature which may have predisposed Paul Newman toward a career in acting. The first was the fact that his father's brother, Uncle Joe, was a newspaperman, a poet and a song-writer. It was he who guided young Paul toward the classics and encouraged the boy to become a voracious reader of poetry, literature, plays, etc. The second influence was Paul's mother, who had a passionate interest in the theatre. She attended the Hanna Theatre in Cleveland regularly and, upon coming home, would describe each play and its players to her younger son.

Needless to say, when Paul himself made his debut onstage, Theresa Newman couldn't have been more thrilled. Paul's first role was a court jester in a grammar school production about Robin Hood. He was seven at the time, and what made his debut special was that Paul sang an original song written by his Uncle Joe. His family and the audience were duly appreciative, but Paul himself said of the experience, 'I felt just as uncomfortable onstage then as I do now.'

Encouraged by his mother, Paul appeared in many school plays. At the age of ten, he played before a large audience at the Cleveland Playhouse in a children's production of *St George and the Dragon*. Paul played St George, while a placid old bulldog played the dragon. The climax of the play came when Paul poured salt on the 'dragon's' tail and vanquished him. Ever in quest of a greater challenge, then as now, Paul recalled, 'I wanted to do the Dragon. It was a much meatier role.'

While attending Shaker Heights High School, Paul Newman both stage-managed and acted in various productions, but to him they were just enjoyable extracurricular pastimes. At that time he had no thoughts of an acting career. In fact, if Newman had attained his full height earlier, he probably would have spent his free time on the playing field instead of the stage. 'I've had to work hard to achieve everything,' Paul said, looking back to that time in particular. 'I was a short, scrawny, 99-pound kid in high school, who couldn't even qualify to try out for the junior varsity football team.'

'I also was too short for Officers Candidate School,' he went on, 'until I grew four inches in one year.' (Paul's height has in fact been the subject of much debate. Some sources say he's 5' 10 ½"; others who know him say he's really only 5' 6".) In fact, one person saw me in my uniform and said, 'Aren't you a little old for Sea Scouts?"'

Short or not, Paul had his good looks, a sharp mind, and considerable charisma. He was able to utilise all of these assets on the school debating team. He had no trouble grabbing the audience's attention and driving his points home with his articulate speech, good timing and skilful delivery. His homelife gave him an advantage here, since in the Newman household lively discussions about politics, the arts, and contemporary issues, as well as family matters, were the norm.

Paul had a quiet side as well. Frequently, during his teen years, he would disappear for hours, going on long, rambling walks in and around Cleveland, with his dog Cleo for company. Whatever Paul thought about during these walks remained his own secret. Even at this time, people who knew him were aware of a certain aura of privacy which Paul maintained.

'The quality of elusiveness, a characteristic of many successful and famous people, is a tantalising trait that excites curiosity in all who encounter it,' Lawrence Quirk, author of *The Films of Paul Newman*, wrote. 'Newman, even then, possessed this quality. People recognised a separateness, a confidence from within that sustained and guided him unaided by friends and family. He was truly independent. A stubbornness and polite defiance began to reveal itself in small ways ... Yet he contained this restlessness, and his loyalties still lay within the conventional expectations of his family and the society in which he lived.'

Perhaps even then Paul Newman suspected in his heart that a special destiny was to be his.

After graduation from high school, Paul's options and

prospects seemed all too mundane. Unwilling to commit himself either to college or a career in his father's sporting goods store, Paul took on the unlikely job of selling encyclopedias door-to-door. Saying that he had taken the job 'to see whether I could sell myself to people,' Paul delighted in the challenge of trying out various sales techniques on his potential customers. Unconsciously using acting skills he didn't even know he possessed, Paul found himself adept at 'playing to' the many personalities and types he encountered. Before long, Paul had amassed a profit of $500, a tidy sum back then, which he proceeded to invest in a theatrical venture. The show flopped, taking with it all of Paul's money.

At loose ends once again, Paul gave in to family pressure and started working as a trainee at his father's store. Arthur Newman, Sr., overly careful not to be accused of favouritism, went to the opposite extreme, paying Paul less than his co-workers and making him come in a half hour earlier and leave a half hour later than the others.

Paul tried hard to please his father, but the truth was that he just didn't enjoy working in a retail business, even if it was owned by his family. The war, which was escalating in the Pacific, provided an outlet for Paul and his unfocused ambitions.

He enlisted in the Navy and, volunteering to be a pilot, was selected for the Naval Air Corps Officers Training Program, to be given at Yale University. Paul was more excited about this opportunity than about anything thus far in his life. He was enthusiastic about the prospect of being a pilot engaged in fighting for his country, and at the same time he was proud to be at a venerable institution like Yale. Unfortunately, this exhilarating period in Paul's life was to last only four months, when it was discovered during a routine physical that he was colour blind.

His dream of being a Navy pilot shattered, Paul was instead assigned to the Air Corps. He served his country as a radioman third class, on torpedo planes and submarine patrols off Guam, Hawaii, and Saipan. Although this was a potentially dangerous assignment, Paul saw no actual combat. 'Those years were spent drinking and reading everything that came into my hands,' he said. 'When I was in Hawaii, Guam and Saipan, I was reading ten or fifteen books per week. Just at the point when I thought I'd see some action, the atomic bomb was dropped and the war was over,' Paul recalled.

Considerably matured by the war years, Newman made use of the G.I. Bill and enrolled at Kenyon College in Gambier, Ohio, then one of the top colleges for men in the country. Only 21 when he started at Kenyon, Paul remembers the ensuing four years as 'the best of my life'. He started as an economics major, but admitting to himself yet again that he found business matters boring, he switched his major to English and speech.

Having attained his full height, and a weight of 150 pounds, Paul was finally able to realise another ambition when he made the second string football team at Kenyon. This accomplishment, coupled with his good looks, made Paul popular with girls for the first time in his life. He 'played the field' in this regard too, not wishing at this point to settle down with any one girl.

In fact, Paul preferred to spend much of his spare time out with the boys, pursuing his second favourite sport after football – beer drinking. His Kenyon class year-book attests to his prowess at this pastime by mentioning that he had received 'magnum cum lager' honours.

As it turned out, Newman's famed thirst for beer, which persists to this day, was at least partly responsible for making him an actor rather than just an English major who also played football. One night when Newman and some of his buddies were out drinking, they got into a bar-room brawl and landed in jail. As punishment for this incident, two of the guys were expelled from Kenyon, and the other four, including Paul, were put on probation and kicked off the football team.

It was at this point that an old pattern repeated itself. In high school, when Paul had been too short and too slight to play football, he had turned to acting in and stage-managing school plays. Now that he could no longer play football at Kenyon, he again thought of the stage as a substitute.

'I hadn't thought about acting in the two years I'd been at Kenyon,' Paul told an interviewer, 'but I had to do something with my spare time, so I went over to the Speech Department, where they were holding auditions for *The Front Page.*'

As it turned out, Paul got the lead role of Hildy Johnson. He went on to appear in nine more productions at Kenyon, including *Charley's Aunt, R.U.R., The Taming of the Shrew,* and *The Alchemist.*

Paul's thespian talents were obvious and he quickly found recognition as an actor. According to his drama professor, James Michael, he remembers having trouble 'not casting Paul as the lead in every play – that's how good he was.'

But Newman, with characteristic self-deprecation, called himself 'probably one of the worst college actors in history . . . I had no idea what I was doing. I learned my lines by rote and simply said them without spontaneity, without any idea of dealing with the forces around me on stage, without knowing what it meant to act and to react. I didn't learn about any of that until I got into the Actors Studio in August, 1952,' he maintained.

It can be deduced that with this statement and others to come, Paul wasn't giving himself enough credit for having been gifted with natural talent. True, he hadn't had professional training, and perhaps he wasn't aware of all the dynamics of his craft, or emotional ramifications of his character. Nevertheless, even in his early twenties, Paul Newman was able to portray complicated roles and display a range of emotion on stage to the satisfaction of both his teachers and his audiences. If, in retrospect it seems to him that 'he didn't know what he was doing', whatever he was doing was good enough for those who watched him perform.

Even back then, Paul Newman was aware of a deeper truth about acting – one which he was going to struggle with for many years. 'I was terrorised by the emotional requirements of being an actor,' he told an interviewer. 'Acting is like letting your pants down. You're exposed.'

In 1948, at the end of his junior year in college, Paul did a summer season at a theatre in Plymouth, Massachusetts. Even then he didn't take acting seriously or think of it as a possible career. 'I didn't have any singleness of purpose about acting until I became successful at it,' Paul said. 'In those early days, I was thinking of becoming a teacher. I more or less stumbled into serious acting. I wanted to run from the sporting goods business, and acting was as good a way as any. People dedicated to an art are usually running *toward* something,' he went on, 'but I was just running away, and where I arrived was the result of a series of accidents.'

The next serendipitous 'accident' that happened to Paul occurred during his senior year at Kenyon. He was offered a 'room and board' scholarship for a summer season at Williams Bay, Wisconsin. Paul's graduation ceremony was on June 13, 1949, at two o'clock in the afternoon. By four o'clock he was on a train bound for Williams Bay.

For the first time in his theatrical experience, Paul had escaped student status. As a fully-fledged member of the professional company, he had the freedom to learn what was rapidly becoming his chosen craft. He not only appeared in plays, but filled in as stage manager and even assistant director. He also eagerly participated in endless discussions about the nature of theatre, the current trends in society, the meaning of art, etc. with his fellow members of the company, who considered Paul their equal and valued his opinions and insights.

It was at this time that Paul started to think seriously about the theatre and what it could mean to him in terms of a career

— not a career that he had chosen simply to run away from the family business, but one that perhaps really suited him. 'Actually,' Paul Newman admitted years later, 'when people start to do something, they *are* heading towards a goal.'

After his summer stint was over, Newman – his acting talent obvious to others, if not himself – was invited to join the Woodstock Players, a year-round theatre group, based in Woodstock, Illinois. This was Paul's most serious venture in the performing arts so far. Between the autumn of 1949 and the spring of 1950, Paul was to appear in no less than seventeen plays put on by this accomplished repertory group. Some of these were *Suspect, Cyrano de Bergerac, The Candlestick Maker, Dark of the Moon, Our Town, Meet Me in St Louis, Mr Roberts* and *Born Yesterday.*

One of his earliest roles with the Woodstock Players was that of the 'Gentlemen Caller' in Tennessee William's classic, *The Glass Menagerie.* Interestingly enough, 38 years later, Paul Newman was to direct his second wife, Joanne Woodward, in this haunting play, in the role of the mother, Amanda. Karen Allen played the crippled daughter and John Malkovich was the 'Gentlemen Caller' in the 1987 film version that received considerable critical acclaim when it was shown at the Cannes Film Festival.

But of all the Woodstock productions he appeared in, a show called *John Loves Mary,* by Norman Krasner, turned out to be the most important to Paul Newman. It was significant not only in terms of his career but in terms of his personal life as well. While Paul portrayed John, a soldier, the role of Mary was played by a young drama student from nearby Lawrence College. She was tall, with blonde hair and brown eyes, and her name was Jacqueline Witte. A romance was about to bloom.

Paul and Jackie not only complemented each other on stage, but in private also. From the start, the pair clicked, feeling an attraction that was both physical and emotional. Jackie was different from the other young women Paul had known. In fact, she seemed like his female counterpart, with her intelligence, wit and articulateness. Besides, she was talented at her craft and an independent thinker. Paul's previous courtship pattern of dating a girl just a few times and then dropping her ceased abruptly when he met Jackie Witte. He found he wanted to spend as much time with her as possible, and each day they made new discoveries about one another.

Never had Paul been able to open up the way he did to Jackie. Never had he felt so close to another human being. It seemed like true love to both of them, and they didn't hold back. As was so common in those pre-Pill days, Jackie became pregnant and the young couple was soon married. Their son Allan Scott (whom everyone always called by his middle name), would be born on September 23, 1950.

Several major life changes took place for Paul Newman in the spring of 1950. Some were happy and some upsetting, but taken together they were more than any 25-year-old could comfortably handle. First Paul became a husband, then a father-to-be. No sooner had he accustomed himself to marriage and impending parenthood than word came that his father was gravely ill. Paul, who had taken a job as a labourer on a farm near Woodstock to supplement his meagre income from the theatre, learned of his father's illness in April. He dropped everything and, taking Jackie with him, returned to Cleveland. By May his father was dead. The sudden and untimely nature of his passing left Paul devastated. He had always longed to be closer to his father, to have the older man understand him, and 'forgive' him for not being business-orientated and not wanting to work at the family sporting goods store.

In actuality, the two were very much alike, since Paul described Arthur Newman, Sr. as 'a brilliant, erudite man' who possessed 'a marvellous, whimsical sense of humour.' He had been hired by the *Cleveland Press* at the age of seventeen, the youngest reporter ever to win a job there, but had later decided to give up this promising career in favour of running the family business.

Evidently not being willing or able to follow in his father's footsteps, even when he had no such promising career to give up, Paul was filled with a certain sense of guilt and inadequacy. He paid a price for straying from paternal expectations. 'I think he always thought of me as pretty much of a lightweight,' Paul said of his father in a *Time* magazine interview. 'He treated me like he was disappointed in me a lot of the time, and he had every right to be.'

Unfortunately, Paul felt that in his father's eyes he was a failure, and with the elder Newman's untimely death, any chance of finally 'proving himself' to his father and winning his approval was ended. To Paul this seemed especially frustrating in light of his subsequent success as a movie actor. Perhaps that is why his repeated failure to garner an Oscar hurt so much.

'It has been one of the great agonies of my life that he could never know,' Paul said. 'I wanted desperately to show him that somehow along the line I could cut the mustard, and I never got a chance.'

However, what the elder Newman wanted was for Paul to remain in Cleveland and learn the sporting goods business from the ground up, like a dutiful son. After all, hadn't he himself made such a sacrifice?

Ironically, after his father's death that is exactly what Paul did — he stayed on in Cleveland and helped to run the store along with his uncle, brother, and cousin. During this emotionally difficult time Paul had Jackie to cling to, and the birth of their son on September 23, 1950, was a welcome antidote to grief for the whole Newman family.

Some months later, the Newman heirs decided to sell the store — and Paul was freed forever of any responsibilities and conflicts in this regard. Rather than leave town with Scott, still a tiny infant, Paul took on some odd jobs. 'One was as manager of a golf range where we picked up golf balls and cleaned them for reuse,' he said, flashing that mischievous famous grin of his. 'I also did a little acting over a local radio station for the McCann-Erickson advertising agency and for the Ohio Bell Telephone Company.' Even in the confines of Cleveland, he had gravitated back to some form of acting.

By the autumn of 1951, Paul decided it was definitely time to move on. With the kind of creative thinking that Newman was to become famous for, which mixed zaniness with practicality, Paul picked up his small family and his even smaller bank account, and moved them to Yale, where he enrolled in the Drama School as a graduate student. Still unwilling or afraid to think in terms of an acting career, Paul intended at this point to earn a Master's degree so that he could eventually teach speech and theatre at the college level, preferably at his alma mater, Kenyon College.

Paul, Jackie, and their infant son settled into an apartment on the top floor of a rambling, three-storey wooden house on a quiet, tree-lined street in New Haven. Back then, it was still a genteel, small town, with the added charm of having the old-fashioned, ivy-covered buildings of Yale in its midst. Living in New Haven and attending Yale, which he'd left so reluctantly almost ten years before because of his colour blindness, Paul became increasingly enamoured of New England. Both the free thinking, urbane attitudes he found in New Haven and the beautiful countryside surrounding it suited him. Later on, he would make Connecticut his home base.

Even though the courses Newman had chosen centred on the dynamics of drama and directing, he was still required to do his share of acting. That first year, Paul appeared in six one-act plays, three full-length ones, and in a major production put on by the Drama School. This was an original play about the life of Beethoven. In it, he played the composer's nephew, 'a very formal guy,' as Paul described him. As usual, he didn't think much of his own performance, but William Leibling, a New York theatrical agent who caught the show, knew talent when he saw it. Although he didn't care for the play, Leibling was so impressed by Paul's performance that he urged him to come to New York and try out for the Broadway stage. If Paul did decide to try for the big time, Leibling told the young actor to be sure and look him up.

Even some of Paul's professors were urging him to give his obvious acting skills a shot rather than settle on a career as a teacher. At that time the New York stage was in a state of flux, welcoming new, innovative ideas. Plays were being imported from Europe and experimental theatres were springing up both on Broadway and off. Paul was also excited to hear about the prestigious Actors Studio in New York. Run by Lee Strasberg, it taught the technique of 'method acting' later made famous by Marlon Brando.

Concerns about providing his family with security rather than subjecting them to the fickle nature of show business still held Paul back. But finally, when Jackie herself urged him to give show business a try, Paul managed to stifle the practical side of his nature and allow the risk-taking, adventurous, hopeful side to take over. He made the final decision in the summer of 1952, and then it was goodbye, New Haven – hello, New York!

The idea of New York had been full of glamour, excitement, and easy success for Paul Newman. The reality of the city hit the 27-year-old actor like a punch in the stomach. First of all, money was tight. The small family couldn't afford to live in Manhattan. Instead, Paul settled Scott and Jackie (now pregnant with their second child) into a $60 dollar a month apartment on Staten Island near Jackie's aunt, who would provide companionship to the young mother, as well as free baby-sitting on the rare occasions when Paul and Jackie could afford a night out.

So there they were, stuck in a strange, out-of-the-way borough that was separated from Manhattan by a large expanse of murky water. He was an unemployed actor – she was pregnant again. To make matters worse, it was one of the hottest summers on record. Paul described a typical day at this time as follows: 'I had one decent suit in those days – an old seersucker – and I'd put it on every morning. I'd start out at eight a.m., take the ferry to Manhattan, make the rounds of the casting agents, follow up all the tips in the trade papers, and then get back to Staten Island in time to peddle encyclopedias.'

But Paul was lucky, because within a month he had landed his first job, a bit part in a television drama called *The March of Time*. The role he was hired to play – that of an old man applauding at the inauguration of President McKinley – hardly seemed suited to a handsome young actor with blonde hair and heart-stopping blue eyes. Still, such are the vagaries of television, and Newman wasn't about to argue with the fee of $75 for a few hours of work.

That first job only enhanced Paul's zeal for acting. Ever thorough and tenacious in his search for work, he managed to get small roles in several TV shows in the next few months, and won a regular role on a TV soap opera, *The Aldwych Family*.

One might well wonder if doing TV shows seemed like a come-down to Paul, who up until then had performed on stage. The answer is no; in fact, Paul revered TV and considered it a stepping stone to the big time.

'When I first came to New York it was a simple joy just to walk along Broadway and feel that, with luck, you might get into the theatrical scene with a really worthwhile part,' Newman recalled. 'Marvellous new plays by people like Rod Serling and Paddy Chayefsky were being performed live on television. Arthur Miller and Tennessee Williams were bringing fresh concepts into drama. It was the kind of action I imagined to have taken place in Elizabethan London,' Paul went on. 'I wanted a piece of that action, and getting into television was the first step.'

Soon Newman became known to all the major networks and

was getting steady work. His face became familiar to viewers through his numerous appearances on such shows as *The Web*, *You Are There*, and *Danger*. One of his more prestigious TV appearances was a starring role in a musical adaptation of Thornton Wilder's *Our Town*. His co-stars were Frank Sinatra and Eva Marie Saint.

Even though regular work in TV made living in New York less financially precarious for Paul and his young family, his ambitions were far from fulfilled. Taking William Leibling at his word, the struggling young actor decided to look the agent up. Leibling not only remembered Paul from his days at Yale but immediately recommended him to noted playwright William Inge, who was then casting for the imminent production of his play, *Picnic*, on Broadway.

Paul described himself as 'scared stiff' at the prospect of reading for the famed playwright. With characteristic self-deprecation, Newman said, 'I thought I read very badly. Then, a month after that, I read for the director, Joshua Logan, and came away with the job of understudying the lead, Ralph Meeker.'

After a few weeks of rehearsal, Newman was offered the supporting male role, that of Alan Seymour, a well-meaning rich boy who loses his girl to his more physically attractive friend. For this he was paid $150 per week, a princely sum back then. His female co-stars were Janice Rule and Kim Stanley, then talented unknowns like himself.

Even more important, the play was a success and Newman's performance won critical acclaim in the top newspapers of the day. Joe Chapman of the *New York Daily News* stated: 'The rich boy was very well played by Paul Newman.' Both the *New York Post* and *New York Daily Mirror* called his portrayal 'excellent'. Brooks Atkinson in the *New York Times* was even more generous in his praise, writing that 'Paul Newman knows how to express the sensitive aspect of the character . . . a college lad infatuated with pretty faces.'

As the song goes, 'it was a very good year' for Paul Newman, both in terms of his career and his personal life. Barely twelve months after his arrival in New York as a total unknown, he had a featured role in a smash hit Broadway show. Not only that, but all of New York's top critics thought he was good! 1953 was also special because Paul and Jackie's first daughter, Susan, was born. And, thanks to his fatter paycheques, Paul was able to move his growing family to a more spacious and comfortable two-bedroom apartment in Queens Village, Long Island.

With all the hustle and bustle surrounding the above events, the hiring of a young actress from Georgia as understudy to both Janice Rule and Kim Stanley in *Picnic* hardly seemed important to Paul Newman. but it would prove to be, because her name was Joanne Woodward.

Chapter 2

Joanne Woodward was also a winter baby, born in Thomasville, Georgia, on February 27, 1930, the temperature was near 70° and the air felt almost balmy. In Thomasville, a small town near the Florida border, it seldom if ever got cold.

A healthy baby, Joanne turned into a bewitching beautiful little girl with blonde hair, inquisitive green eyes and a pixie face. Joanne was an affectionate, sensitive, intelligent child who was gifted with a vivid imagination. She was outgoing and eager to please, but she also possessed an independent streak and knew her own mind early on. When Joanne wanted her own way it wasn't because she was spoiled, it was because she really felt that her way of doing things was right. From the start, she was her own person.

For instance, as Joanne told a reporter, 'I was interested in pigtails rather than curls . . . so I snipped off the ringlets on my Shirley Temple doll.'

Her childhood in the sleepy Southern town with its balmy climate was pleasant, almost idyllic. Joanne did the usual things, including piano and ballet lessons, plus more tomboyish pursuits which she enjoyed. She did well in school and was discovered to have a particularly high I.Q.

Everything was fine – until the bottom fell out of her world. Suddenly, and for reasons still unknown, Joanne's mother sought a divorce from her father, Wade Woodward, an attractive and highly intelligent man who later became a vice president of Scribners, the well-known publishing company.

Joanne, who adored her father, was devastated. The rift was all the more painful because, after the divorce, her father moved away, and Joanne saw him only rarely. She missed her father acutely all through her childhood, and it was only later, through therapy undertaken as an adult, that she was able to come to terms with this deep and abiding loss.

It's ironic that, having suffered so much pain through divorce as a child, the love of Joanne's life turned out to be a married man who could be with her only at the cost of divorcing his own wife.

Fortunately, Joanne received lots of love and attention from her gentle, doting mother. Although Joanne was and still is adamant about not discussing her private life – especially her deeper feelings – with interviewers, there is reason to believe the Joanne was lonely, perhaps even unhappy, for much of her childhood. Then as now, however, she kept these feelings to herself and sought solace in books (progressing from popular novels to great works of literature) and also in her own fertile and creative imagination. No doubt young Joanne acted out many a dramatic scene in the privacy of her own room, or along with her friends.

Hollywood films, which provided so many Americans with a welcome escape from the ravages of the Great Depression, were a frequent source of pleasure and entertainment for Joanne and her mother.

A film based on the life of Madame Curie which starred Greer Garson made such an impression on Joanne as a child that she wanted to be a doctor. But it wasn't long before the insightful child realised that it was the acting in the film rather than its subject matter that had beguiled her – and she changed her career choice accordingly.

At the age of nine, Joanne attended an event that eclipsed everything in her life so far in terms of excitement and inspiration, and resulted in a flash of insight about her own future. The event was the Southern premiere of *Gone With the Wind*, at which Joanne and her mother were fortunate enough to be present. But besides taking in the wonder and majesty of the film itself, the occasion was special in another way which Mrs. Woodward well remembers.

'She (Joanne) was so excited, she kept jumping up and down in her seat when Vivien Leigh, as Scarlett O'Hara, came on the screen,' her mother recalled. 'Joanne would point her finger at her and tell me in a stage whisper, 'I shall be a great actress one day.' You know something? She was so convincing that I believed her, even though she wasn't anywhere near ten years old.'

Joanne was lucky to have a mother who took her ambitions seriously instead of scoffing at them. The creative spark which the young girl felt within her was allowed to grow, fuelled by the films she saw, the books and plays she read – and most of all by Joanne's creative imagination and her strong determination to become an actress of note when she grew up.

When Joanne was 15, the family moved to Greenville, South Carolina. There Joanne received more encouragement, as well as some valuable dramatic coaching, from her high school speech and drama teacher, Albert Maclain. To this day she remains grateful to him for taking her acting ambitions seriously and further fanning the creative fire within her. Not that all the high school productions she appeared in were 'serious theatre'. In fact, one of her most memorable roles was as 'Lady Make-Believe', an animated doll.

By this time, Joanne had turned into something of a 'living doll' herself. A little over five feet, four inches tall, she weighed 117 pounds and sported a petite but curvaceous figure which before long would be described in gossip columns as 34-24-34. Although her blonde-haired, green-eyed good looks and quiet but charismatic personality attracted a lot of male attention, Joanne did not allow herself to be diverted from her first love, which was acting.

After high school she attended Louisiana State University, where she lasted two years. College courses didn't seem to make sense in terms of her brilliantly burning ambition to be not just an actress, but a famous actress. Even as an undergraduate, she was cast as Ophelia in the University's production of *Hamlet,* and performed the role to universal acclaim.

The summer after her sophomore year, Joanne returned to Greenville, where she appeared in a theatre production of *The Glass Menagerie,* a play which the young Paul Newman had once appeared in, and a play which would become important to both of them in future years. This first taste of the theatre only whetted Joanne's appetite for more. Returning to college was unthinkable. The lights of Broadway beckoned, shining as brightly as her own talent and ambition. And somehow Joanne, with her limited funds and her even more limited experience in the 'real world,' managed to convince her mother that New York was where she should be.

They say that timing is everything, and Joanne Woodward's timing in this case was impeccable. She had definitely arrived in the right place at the right time. Conditions in New York had never been better for attractive, talented young people who also had the ambition and *chutzpah* to pound the pavements, knock on doors and sell themselves to casting agents, acting coaches, producers, etc.

When she arrived in New York at the age of 21, Joanne's first priority was to get the best dramatic taining available. She signed up with the Neighbourhood Playhouse, a dramatic workshop which had the reputation of training many young students who went on to achieve stardom. Through the Neighbourhood Playhouse and then the Actors Studio (where Newman also studied), Joanne was to meet many talented hopefuls who, like herself, would soon become major Hollywood stars and household names.

Meantime, these talented newcomers had to eat and pay rent, and a large number of them (including first Paul Newman and then Joanne) found work on the many series and specials being produced for live TV.

Many of the shows were broadcast from the RCA Building at Rockefeller Centre. Upon going there in the company of an interviewer several years ago and noticing the Commodore Drug Store, Joanne Woodward's thoughts flashed back to 1951 when she first came to New York from Greenville. 'I spent hours here, sipping coffee with Rod Steiger and Jimmy Dean,' Joanne recalled. 'We were doing live television then. I was doing soap operas and the Robert Montgomery Theatre. I almost became a tour guide, but was saved from that, luckily.'

Joanne was saved from subsistence jobs such as tour guide and waitress by that persistently burning ambition of hers. Her goals drove her not only to take acting classes, but to try out for almost every TV show available. At the same time, lots of Broadway shows were opening, and Joanne trained herself to watch the papers for cast calls and open auditions. To audition for a show, she had to prepare a dramatic piece, plus make sure her clothes, hairstyle and make-up looked right.

Assiduously and without complaining, Joanne did all of the above and more. Eventually her efforts paid off. Somehow she heard that one of the hit plays on Broadway was in need of a female understudy. She auditioned and was promptly hired to understudy both Janice Rule and Kim Stanley in *Picnic*. This was Broadway, and as close as she'd come so far to the big time. Joanne was so dizzy with a mixture of fear and excitement that she hardly had time to notice the guy who played the second male lead, except that his name was Paul and he had piercing blue eyes.

Coincidentally, Newman himself had started out in *Picnic* as an understudy for Ralph Meeker, who played the sexually magnetic leading character. The play ran for 14 months, and at one point when Meeker went on vacation, Newman took over his part. On the strength of that performance, Paul asked the director of the play, Josh Logan, if he could assume Meeker's role when *Picnic* went on the road.

The answer Logan gave hit Newman like a blow to the solar plexus, and it was certainly a blow to his ego. 'Josh told me no, because I didn't carry any sexual threat,' Newman recalled wryly. 'At that particular point, I probably didn't,' he admitted. 'That sort of thing has a lot to do with conviction.'

When Paul asked the great director what he could do to improve his animal magnetism, Logan advised him to 'get in shape'. 'The way I translated that was six hours in the gym every day,' Newman said. Meantime he went to work on his manner with the ladies as well as his muscles. 'You can measure each woman,' Paul explained, 'and find ways of being gallant, of listening, of crowding, of pursuing.'

Paul probably learned this technique and others through his training at the Actors Studio, which accepted him around this time. His teachers, Lee Strasberg and Elia Kazan, were acknowledged masters of the craft but his classmates turned out to be no less impressive. These included James Dean, Karl Malden, Geraldine Page, Kim Stanley, Rod Steiger, Eli Wallach, Maureen Stapleton and Julie Harris.

Duly impressed by his fellow students even before they became superstars, Paul said, 'Man, I just sat back there and watched how people did things and had enough sense not to open my big mouth.'

What Paul and the others were learning was Strasberg's famous 'Method' of acting, which demanded that an actor 'become' the part he is playing. It's a way of acting from the inside out, and each performer of the Method is expected to draw on his or her memory, experience, and feelings in order to project the various emotions of the character being portrayed.

This process was difficult, at times gruelling, for Paul. 'I had a lot to overcome,' he recalled. 'I discovered that I was primarily a cerebral actor, as I still am. I began to understand that actors who are instinctively emotional are much luckier. The instinctively emotional actor – like Geraldine Page, Kim Stanley, Marlon Brando, and also my wife (to be) Joanne – work, I think, from the inside out. Their emotional equipment is much more readily available to them.'

Still, Paul Newman found that learning the Method was invaluable to him not only in terms of making him a better actor, but also in terms of putting him in closer touch with his personal emotions. At that time even more than now, males in our society were trained to be 'strong', not only physically but also in terms of controlling their emotions. It was unthinkable for a man to cry, especially with others around. Males learned early to hide any emotion that could be considered 'weak' or 'feminine.' Some males learned this lesson so well that they ignored or denied powerful emotions and, zombie-like, weren't even aware of their own feelings.

At any rate, once he became more relaxed at the Actors Studio, Paul found himself able to rediscover many 'lost' emotions from his past. And while this process was sometimes painful, it ended up by giving him a wholeness and a range of feelings that he hadn't been in touch with before. At the Studio, Paul also made many lasting friendships with his fellow actors and actresses.

By far the most significant friendship Newman formed at this time was with the young blonde-haired, green-eyed Southern actress who was understudying the two leading female roles in *Picnic*. From a casual acquaintance born of working together, Paul and Joanne progressed to a real friendship which revolved around their common interests. Having both been voracious readers as youngsters, they had endless books, plays and poetic works to discuss. Both were attending the Actors Studio, and this gave them another shared interest. Many hours were spent by this pair over coffee or beers, discussing Method acting and the amazing way it had of dredging up long-buried emotions and forcing you not only to feel them, but use them in your work. They often shared an inexpensive lunch or dinner together before or after their *Picnic* performances, and sometimes they took in a movie or play – most often to see the work of someone they knew or admired.

Their personalities complemented each other's, Paul being brash and outspoken, and Joanne being introspective and intuitive, but filled with intense feelings and convictions. They were intellectually well matched and were always making each other laugh with witty, ironic remarks.

They called themselves friends, but even back then it was something more. Yet, each night Paul went home to his family in Queens Village and Joanne went home to her own apartment. Paul had no desire to put his marriage in jeopardy, and Joanne didn't want him to. If at times they felt an undeniable sexual attraction for each other, they simply ignored it. For a while, this method actually worked.

What worked even better was Paul leaving town. This he did early in 1954 after Warner Bros. offered him a long-term contract at $1,000 per week. Soon after *Picnic* closed, he left for Hollywood, leaving Jackie and the kids on Long Island. Not knowing how long he'd be gone or what he'd be doing on the West Coast, he didn't want to uproot his family.

Almost from the start, Paul's worst fears about the Hollywood movie industry were realised. Like most of his fellow students at the Actors Studio, he disapproved of the Hollywood studio system that bought, sold, packaged and merchandised newcomers like so many pieces of meat. Talent and artistic integrity were valueless out there; all the studio heads cared about was whether something would 'sell'.

Still, the money the film industry was willing to pay was hard to pass up, and Paul knew that many of the best actors and actresses worked in films, in spite of their negative attitudes toward Hollywood. They had managed to make money without 'selling their souls' to the system. Some actors, such as Humphrey Bogart, Kirk Douglas and Jack Lemmon, had become top Hollywood legends and managed to keep their own identities and values intact even while living within the very jaws of the Hollywood star-maker machine. But all too many others had allowed the Hollywood machinery to turn them into performing monkeys or completely fictitious characters created by the all-powerful movie publicity departments. Seduced by surface glamour, swimming pools, easy sex, beach-front estates and the luxurious material possessions, these paper doll creatures who were the figments of other people's fantasies and imaginations drifted through life, often becoming alcoholics, drug addicts, or both.

From the start, Paul Newman vowed he wouldn't allow Hollywood to destroy him, but he also saw almost immediately that maintaining his independence and integrity would be a struggle. Not that he was in danger of being drawn into the overly lavish but vapid lifestyle he saw all around him. No, Paul's fight would be against the misuse of his talent or any attempted bastardising of his identity. He didn't want Hollywood to make him into anything he was not – and from the start that is exactly what they tried to do.

After a ludicrous screen test during which some cigar-chomping men in business suits stared coldly at him, obviously far from impressed, Paul was sent to the studio hairdressing department, where they made his hair blonder. Within a few days, he was informed that he had been cast in his first film, *The Silver Chalice,* a costume drama about the conflicts between pagans and Christians in ancient Rome. Suddenly Newman found himself in front of the cameras togged out in what he described as a 'cocktail gown'.

His role as a Greek slave named Basil included such lines as 'Helena, is it really you? What a joy!' As Newman soon realised, he had been cast in the film not because of any acting talent on his part, but because of his blue eyes, well-developed physique, and his supposed resemblance to Marlon Brando.

As it turned out, with lines like the above, Paul's acting ability was beside the point.

To this day, Paul enjoys reciting a line from *The New Yorker's* 1954 review of the film: 'Paul Newman delivers his lines with the emotional fervour of a Putnam Division (train) conductor announcing local stops.'

And, according to Joanne Woodward, 'It was the only time an actor played a role without lifting his head. You couldn't even see his blue eyes.'

In Paul's mind, the reason for this was partly due to the embarrassment he felt at being in the film at all, and partly because he was self-conscious about his 'skinny legs' and the costume he wore exposed them.

Paul refused to see *The Silver Chalice* when it came out – until a group of ten friends dragged him to a showing of it in an all-night Philadelphia movie theatre. Even four cases of beer, lugged in for the occasion, weren't enough to soften the blow to Paul about how horrible both the movie – and his performance – were. Ten years later when what is known in the Newman family as 'The Worst Picture Ever Made' was scheduled for a week-long run on Los Angeles TV, Paul took out a large black-bordered ad in both the local daily papers which read 'Paul Newman Apologizes Every Night This Week.'

Although in retrospect *The Silver Chalice* experience has its humorous elements, at the time it was truly excruciating to Paul. 'It was god-awful,' he recalled. 'It's kind of a distinction to say I was in the worst film to be made in the entire 1950s. Everybody kept saying, "How can you go wrong in your first part, starring in a $4 ½ million picture?" Well, three weeks after we started shooting, I called my agent in New York screaming desperately for him to get me a play. I figured the picture would kill me. I wasn't at all sure that I would survive as an actor.'

Luckily for Paul's state of mind at the time, his agent *was* able to find him a featured role in *The Desperate Hours*, a suspenseful, exciting play by Joseph Hayes. Soon to open on Broadway, the drama concerns three escaped convicts who take over the home of a middle class couple with two children and terrorise them as they wait for their get-away money to come through. Newman played the part of sinister Glenn Griffin, ringleader (later to be played on screen by Humphrey Bogart). In the play, Griffin, who hated his father, transfers this enmity to his helpless victim, played by Karl Malden. The role was a challenging one for Paul and gave him a chance to utilise his training in Method acting.

Newman got his best reviews yet. Brooks Atkinson of the *New York Times* wrote: 'Paul Newman plays the boss thug with a wildness that one is inclined to respect. The play shatters the nerves. There could be no more stir-crazy and animal-crafty desperado than Newman.'

The show's rave reviews and graphic descriptions of handsome Paul Newman as a 'bad guy' captured the attention of females in particular. For the first time Paul was besieged by screaming groups of women outside the stage door each night when he left the theatre.

The Desperate Hours ran for eight months, during which time *The Silver Chalice* was released, to predictably bad reviews. Trying not to think about what Warner Bros. might call upon him to do next — that is, if they still wanted to keep him under contract — Paul kept himself busy attending the Actors Studio twice a week and again working in live television. He received special praise for his performances in two television plays, *Bang the Drum Slowly* and *The Five Fathers of Pepe.*

'Television dramas were exciting and vibrant in those days — because they were live,' Newman said in a *Playboy* interview some years later. 'Men like Tad Mosel and Paddy Chayefsky and Max Shulman were writing for television, and they made it an inventive era. Call it kitchen sink, inner search, what have you — it was great ... That whole glorious period of television has disappeared,' he went on, 'and nothing has come along to replace it.'

Finally the expected call came from Hollywood, and it wasn't good news. Because *The Silver Chalice* was a box office flop, Warner's was altering the original contract they had offered Paul. Besides the two films a year for five years he had to appear in, the film studio would also have the option of signing him to a third film. However, now that Warner Bros. had Newman locked up, they had no suitable parts for him.

Metro-Goldwyn-Mayer Studios then offered to buy part of Paul's contract. The second film of his career, *The Rack*, was with Metro. In it, Paul portrayed a young Army captain who is on trial for treason when he is broken by Chinese communist brainwashing techniques. Paul was pleased with the film, which was sensitively and powerfully written by Rod Serling and Stewart Stern, and felt that he'd turned in a creditable performance. So did the critics, but as Paul himself put it, 'nobody went to see it.'

His next film, also done through Metro-Goldwyn-Mayer, came about through a tragic stroke of fate. On September 30, 1955, Paul received word that his old friend James Dean had been killed in a car crash. Newman was devastated, especially since he was to have started working with Dean in a TV version of Hemingway's *The Battler*, in just a few weeks' time.

Out of respect for his friend, Paul was all set to drop the project, but then the producer begged him to take on the title role, which James Dean was to have played. *The Battler* is about a fighter who goes from being an undefeated champ in his twenties, to a violent prison inmate in this thirties, ending up as a punch-drunk bum at the age of forty. Though haunted by the death of his friend, Newman still managed to turn in an excellent performance which was broadcast all across the country.

After the show, the producer, Fred Coe, took Newman and the other cast members out for drinks. The mood in the bar grew merrier and rowdier as the night wore on. Suddenly a short guy who had seen *The Battler* began to heckle Newman. One thing led to another, and 'Shorty' challenged Paul to a fight. A full-fledged brawl ensued, and by the end of it the actor's face was bruised and he had a black eye.

As luck would have it, the next day Paul's agent had scheduled him for a meeting with renowned director Robert Wise and his producer Charles Schnee. They had been planning a film based on the life of heavy-weight boxing champion Rocky Graziano and had wanted James Dean to star in it. After the young actor's tragic death, they had put their film project on hold – until catching Paul Newman's TV performance in *The Battler*. Now they were interested in him as a replacement, and they wanted to see him right away.

Paul had no choice but to show up, black eye and all. 'I walked into the office wearing an eye shade underneath a pair of dark glasses,' he recalled. 'There were several important people in the office, and my entrance caused a bit of stir. "What happened?" the producer asked. "Why are you wearing that shade and those glasses?" I said, 'You know where I got hit in the show last night?" Newman waited for the men to nod assent, then went on, 'Well, we put a bit too much realism into it – and this is the result."

It's said that this supposed willingness on Newman's part to 'go above and beyond the call of duty' for the sake of realism weighed in his favour. At any rate, he was given the starring role in *Somebody Up There Likes Me*.

Paul couldn't have been more pleased. He knew that a lot of thought had gone into the project; he trusted Wise and Schnee to follow through and make a good film. The time was right for a movie about a boy from a deprived background making good; he felt the story would appeal to the public. The role itself appealed to Newman; he looked forward to the challenge of portraying a real character instead of a ridiculous caricature like Basil, the Greek slave.

Again for *Somebody Up There Likes Me*, Paul was 'lent' to Metro-Goldwyn-Mayer. While he liked the film this time, it didn't seem fair to Paul that Warner Bros. was paying him his weekly salary of $1,000 while they were receiving $75,000 per film for renting him out. For an independent person like Paul Newman, the feeling of being 'owned' by a Hollywood studio and forced to appear in any film they decided upon was not a good one. However, at this early stage of his career, he decided not to try to fight the 'system'.

In order to prepare for the film, Paul spent two weeks with Graziano. He observed the fighter's gestures and mannerisms, watched him box, and talked to him for hours on end about his life and experiences. Rocky told Paul what it was like to grow up in a tough, poor neighbourhood with a drunken, abusive father, and also what it was like to struggle, to train, to excel and finally to become a winner.

Paul stresses, however, that he didn't try to mimic Graziano, but to interpret him. 'I didn't try to imitate him in the part,' Newman said. 'I tried to find a balance between him and me − him as the part and the part in me. I tried to play *a* Graziano, not *the* Graziano.'

Besides taking mental notes on the real Rocky, Newman had to prepare for the role physically as well. He went through gruelling daily work-out sessions at the Hollywood gym, training with professional boxers, and learned all the right moves and techniques within the ring.

By the time filming began, Newman was raring to go. He was in peak physical condition, and he hoped to be in top form as an actor too. From the beginning, Paul had had a good feeling about this film, as if 'somebody up there liked *him*' as well. As an added bonus, he and director Robert Wise got along well together. Their talents meshed to bring forth a work they could both be proud of.

The good feeling Newman had abour the film proved to be well-founded. The next summer it was released to rave reviews, receiving accolades not only for script and direction, but for the 'raw power' and 'characterisational integrity' which Paul Newman brought to the part. The film turned him into an overnight sensation and the year's brightest new star.

The film went a long way to giving the young actor an identity of his own, apart from his good looks and the Marlon Brando comparisons which had plagued him up until then. As *Variety's* review put it: 'For Newman *Somebody Up There Likes Me* is a showcasing that should remove the Brando look-alike handicap. His talent is large and flexible.'

Meantime, Paul had something of a more pleasant nature to feel proud of. The same year that he made *Somebody Up There Likes Me*, 1955, also marked the birth of his and Jackie's third child, a girl named Stephanie. After the film finished, Paul was glad to leave Hollywood and return to his family on Long Island. He knew how much they needed him and how much Jackie had missed him during her pregnancy. It hadn't been easy for her, alone except for Scott, now five, and Susan, three. It hadn't been easy for him in Hollywood, either, but he knew that separations were necessary if he wanted to build a film career and earn good money. Now it felt good to be free of the pressures of Hollywood. And, although life in a two-bedroom apartment with two toddlers and an infant was far from serene and stress-free, home was where he was loved and needed, where he felt safe.

Home in the East was definitely a refuge from Hollywood, especially now that Joanne Woodward was out there. Paul tried to concentrate on being a husband and father and forget that other kind of love – made up of friendship, and yes, passion – which, thrown together again in Hollywood, he and Joanne could no longer deny.

Chapter 3

In an uncanny way, Paul Newman's and Joanne Woodward's lives had run parallel. Arriving in New York City within a year of each other, they had both found work on live TV, both studied at the Actors Studio, and both been hired for the Broadway show, *Picnic*. Similarly, while Paul was offered a contract by Warner Bros. and left for Hollywood early in 1954, Joanne signed up with 20th Century Fox and arrived in Hollywood later that year.

In rapid succession, Joanne made three films for Fox: *Count Three and Pray*, *A Kiss Before Dying*, and *No Down Payment*. While the films were good experience for Joanne, enabling her to try out and demonstrate her acting range (in the first she played a boisterous, tomboyish type and in the third a suburban housewife), none of the films was a commercial success. Even more disappointing to Joanne was the fact that none of the films was an artistic achievement for her as an actress. Still, Joanne had the satisfaction of knowing that she had done the best acting job possible within the limited range of each movie.

Like Paul, Joanne was well aware of the pitfalls and abuses posed by the Hollywood star system and had no intention of giving in to them. She knew she would maintain her artistic integrity or she would leave Hollywood.

According to J.C. Landry, author of *Paul Newman*, 'From the start she (Joanne) was adamant about the way in which her career should be managed, refusing to act out the publicity pin-up/starlet charade. Many intelligent Hollywood actresses before her, such as Frances Farmer and Hildegarde Neff, had been destroyed by such nonconformity. Hollywood responded badly to individualists, automatically labelling them 'troublemakers'. But such was the power and effect of Miss Woodward's forceful argument that even the most feared studio bosses were known to yield. She usually succeeded in getting her own way and, more often than not, it was the right one.'

Whether her independent, uncompromising attitudes would ultimately have been damaging to her career is something that will never be clear, because Joanne Woodward's next film, *Three Faces of Eve*, turned out to be one of the biggest hits of all time.

Three Faces of Eve was based on the life of a real woman who was the subject of a clinical study by a pair of doctors, Corbett H. Thigpen and Hervey M. Cleckley. The real 'Eve' was a normal, even drab, small-town housewife besieged with what is known as multiple personalities in psychiatric jargon. A second personality, a far cry from the lacklustre Eve, was that of a vulgar, sexually promiscuous woman, fond of foul language and hard drinking. In control of Eve's mind and body, this second personality goes off on wild sprees which Eve cannot remember afterward. Under stresses like this, her marriage breaks up and Eve enters therapy. The rest of the film centres on the doctors' efforts to come to terms with Eve's personalities, including a third one, more balanced and sensible than the other two, which also emerges.

The script, written by Nunnally Johnson (who also produced and directed the film for Fox) was excellent, but even so, actresses, including Judy Garland and Carroll Baker, turned down the opportunity to play Eve. Evidently the idea of portraying three characters at once was too intimidating, and perhaps the proposed film in script form did not appear to have much potential as a commercial success. It was definitely a project which depended on an excellent actress in the title role; otherwise it could easily turn into a travesty, a melodrama of the worst order, or both.

Fortunately Joanne Woodward and *Three Faces of Eve* came face to face. If there was ever a challenge for a young actress, this was it. She was perfect for the film, and the film was perfect for her. Joanne understood this intuitively, and when she was given the leading role in *Three Faces of Eve,* she felt as if she had been given a rare and precious gift. Perhaps Joanne experienced the same kind of breathless excitement she had felt on that long ago childhood day when she told her mother, 'I'm going to be a great actress someday!'

If so, her feeling would have been appropriate, because *Three Faces of Eve* established Joanne Woodward as one of the greatest actresses of our time. In this *tour de force* performance, the young actress breathed life into all three of Eve's personalities, making each seem distinct and convincingly real. The audience shares Eve's terror at the psychological condition which has taken control of her. Viewers care about her fate so much that even the gruelling sessions between Eve and her psychiatrist (played by Lee J Cobb) are fascinating even to laymen as the two grope for the reason behind Eve's illness and the key to her recovery.

'I was only 14 or 15 when I saw *Three Faces of Eve,* ' says a TV and movie script writer in Hollywood, 'but it left a lasting impression. I was sexually inexperienced, had never heard of schizophrenia, had no real idea of what psychiatry was all about – and yet I was totally able to follow the film and understand what it meant on several different levels. I'm sure this was because of Joanne Woodward and her incredible skill as an actress. I remember a scene of her sitting in a chair, and just by shifting her body around and changing the expressions on her face – suddenly she was a different person. It was eerie the way she did it, really. I'm 45 now and I've never forgotten it,' she confessed.

Ironically, at first Joanne had no idea of the powerful

performance she had given in *Three Faces of Eve* and wondered at her wisdom in taking the film assignment to begin with. 'It was offered to me after June Allyson and Susan Hayward and Judy Garland had rejected it,' Joanne pointed out. 'I cried when I saw the rough cut. I thought my career was ruined.'

As everyone realises now, quite the opposite happened. When *Three Faces of Eve* was released, all of Hollywood sat up and took notice of Joanne Woodward's brilliant performance. Though a virtual unknown, she won the Academy Award for best actress of 1957.

Meantime it was 1956, and while Joanne was filming *Three Faces of Eve*, Paul was busy fulfilling his Warner Bros. contract by making two more less than lustrous movies. The first, with Newman yet again on loan to Metro-Goldwyn-Mayer, was *Until They Sail*. In this tear-jerker, whch turned out to be popular with women movie-goers, Newman played a young Marine captain who is embittered by a broken marriage until he meets and falls in love with a lonely war widow, played by Jean Simmons.

The second movie, *The Helen Morgan Story* (through Warner Bros.), featured Paul as a gangster and bootlegger who treats his girlfriend, Helen Morgan (Ann Blyth), like dirt before turning over a new leaf. These films broke new ground for Newman, in that they were both 'love stories', with the plots centring mainly around the interaction between Paul and his leading ladies. The result was that by the end of 1957, the year they were released, Newman had gained stature as a matinee idol as well as a good actor.

With both Paul and Joanne in Hollywood making movies, it was natural for them to renew the close friendship they had shared in New York. With the uncanny way their careers ran parallel, yet intersecting over and over again, it was impossible for them to keep apart even if they wanted to. It almost seemed as if Fate had stepped in, bringing them together, telling them that they belonged with each other

Paul's good looks soon turned him into a Hollywood sex symbol.

Joanne in an early television drama.

Paul with Ann Blyth in *The Helen Morgan Story*.

A scene from *The Silver Chalice* made in 1954. From left to right, David Stewart, Alex Scourby, Pier Angeli and Paul Newman.

Joanne's performance in *The Three Faces of Eve* won her an Academy Award in 1957.

after all, even though Paul was married.

'Paul and Joanne seemed to be in love during this time,' says an old friend who wishes to remain anonymous. 'Anyone who was around them could tell they were crazy about each other – and I was around them a lot.

'Another young married couple hung out with us too. She was a script girl and he was a stuntman, and they were lots of fun, really down to earth. The three of us, or the five of us, or whatever combination always had loads of fun. We'd always take at least two cars, and then we'd go on little 'excursions' to out-of-the-way places. We never failed to have a good time.

'Our favourite thing was to find a restaurant somewhere up the coast that overlooked the ocean. If it had a beach, so much the better, and if it had fishing, so much the better. One way or another we'd spend the afternoon palling around.

'I tell you, it was beautiful to watch them together. They couldn't keep their eyes off each other – and such beautiful eyes they both had, hers green and slanted like a cat's and his blue like the sky or sea – and they couldn't keep from touching each other. It was hand-holding, and face-stroking, and hugging. But it was earthy too, like him giving her a little squeeze here and a little slap there. They didn't flaunt it – they just felt it.'

Unfortunately, after the first intoxicating months, the lovers had to leave Cloud Nine and come back down to reality. And the reality was that Paul was already married to someone else. The fact was, as much as he was in love, Newman wasn't a philandering type. It wasn't as if he had come out to Hollywood as a handsome young screen stud and picked up a pretty young starlet just for the fun of it. The truth was, he still loved his wife, even if they had grown apart in recent years because of his success. It wasn't as if he had 'outgrown' Jackie and gone in search of someone more exciting. What had happened between himself and Joanne Woodward was unplanned and unexpected. It had started simply because of their common interests, but what developed went way beyond any logical explanation. It was something he had never dreamed of sharing with another human being, something which he never even knew existed. It was mental, physical and spiritual all at once. There was a term which went part of the way to explain it: soul-mates. But then there was the physical aspect of their attraction too, which finally they'd given in to.

In New York it had been easier to fight their growing attraction, because Paul's family was there and he was expected to go home every night. But in Hollywood, each was alone and lonely, until they saw each other – two old friends from New York stuck in Hollywood, a town whose empty values and ostentatious wealth both of them detested. Both were also having problems dealing with the 'studio system' which saw talent as money and used actors as chips in a high-stakes movie game called Hollywood Roulette. They were going through the same things at the same time and there was so much to talk about, so many new feelings and ideas to share.

Was it any wonder they reached out for one another? Being together felt so natural, so right. The old magic came back, only more so, and finally they couldn't deny any longer that it was love. And, being madly, passionately in love, they couldn't deny the physical part any longer either.

And now that Paul and Joanne felt all that for each other, the next logical step was for them to get married and be together always. At that time, in the 1950s, divorce was still considered quite a scandal – and so was living together. And even though Paul and Joanne were rebels in some ways, they were sensitive and honourable where other people's feelings were concerned. In order to marry Joanne, Paul would have to divorce Jackie and leave three innocent children.

As for Joanne, as much as she wanted to be with the man she loved, she couldn't bear the thought of being 'the other woman' in a messy divorce case and being labelled a 'home-wrecker' if the story caused a public scandal, which it probably would. Joanne didn't worry about these things because of her career or 'image'. She worried about hurting Jackie and Paul's children.

Her parents' divorce had been the most painful event of her own childhood, and now the thought that she might be responsible for bringing this same pain to other children was a torment to Joanne. She hadn't set out to fall in love with a married man. It had been just friendship, and like Paul she had done her best to keep it from turning into anything more. But like Paul she had succumbed; together they had allowed themselves to be swept away, and it was ecstasy . . . that is, until the agony of guilt set in.

For all of these reasons, after enjoying a brief time together as lovers in every sense of the word, Paul and Joanne decided to stop seeing each other. It was the only right and decent thing to do, because their love was too hurtful to others. The decision was meant to be final.

Paul was supposed to go back to his wife and children – when he was in New York, that is. At that point, he didn't feel that his film career was assured enough to warrant uprooting his family; besides he said that he didn't want his kids growing up in Hollywood, a place he still held with a certain amount of contempt. There is evidence to suggest that the supposed reconciliation with Jackie didn't go so well. Most likely she had heard about her husband's affair and felt too much resentment to open her arms to him and tell him that all was forgiven.

Estranged from Joanne and feeling alienated from his wife and children, Paul Newman entered the worst phase of his life. He had never known unhappiness and despair of this magnitude, and he didn't know how to deal with it. Usually outgoing and optimistic to the point of being happy-go-lucky, Paul's personality changed. He became extremely moody and withdrew from other people. He drank more than he ever had, and once he got drunk he became aggressive to the point of picking fights.

There were other changes too. According to an acquaintance who knew Paul at this time, he also became promiscuous sexually for the first time in his life. 'Paul was real unhappy after he broke up with Joanne,' this source reveals. 'He was drinking a whole lot, and he'd drink to the point where he didn't give a shit about anything. Where before Paul was really shy with the women, just smiling or laughing shylike at the ones who'd try to pick him up, at this time he started going home with any bimbo who gave him the eye. He had a lot of one-night flings at this time — it helped him to forget, like the drinking. See, he felt like he'd lost his family, he'd lost Joanne, and so nothing mattered but to blot out the pain and get through another night.'

When his film schedule permitted, Paul would return to New York and his family. Even if he and Jackie weren't getting along that well, at least there was some comfort in seeing his kids. But it came to the point where Paul couldn't control his emotions — or his drinking — no matter where he was. Things reached a crisis on the night of July 7, 1956, when he was pulled over by the police in Mineola, Long Island, and charged with leaving the scene of an accident and going through a red light. The 'accident' wasn't serious — Newman had damaged a fire hydrant and some shrubbery with his car — but he made matters worse by giving the officers a hard time. *Somebody Up There Likes Me* had just been released, and as the story goes, Newman, drunk as a skunk, got out of his car, fists clenched, and said to Patrolman Rocco Caggiano, 'I'm acting for Rocky Graziano. What do you want?' Patrolman Caggiano came back with, 'Well, I'm Rocky too, and you're under arrest, pal.'

The upshot was that Newman was handcuffed and brought to the police station where he spent the night in a jail cell. That incident seems to have had a chastening effect on Paul Newman. At any rate, it wasn't too long afterwards that he got hold of himself, and decided to do something about the heavy drinking that was having an increasingly negative effect on his life. Feeling overwhelmed by his problems, he had turned to booze in an attempt to blot them out; now excessive drinking had become a problem in itself. But Paul Newman was damned if he'd let booze get the better of him. Self-destructiveness wasn't really his thing. He had a lot of strength inside him, but somehow his confused emotions had taken control. Now he decided he needed help in sorting them out.

To Paul's way of thinking, consulting a psychoanalyst was a logical and practical decision. If your car was messed up, you consulted a mechanic. Similarly, he reasoned, if your thoughts and emotions were screwed up, you went to a psychiatrist. He had no sense of embarrassment at seeking psychological help.

As it turned out, the experience was helpful beyond his wildest expectations, and to this day he recommends psychotherapy to others. 'What measure of serenity I have in my life is the direct result of analysis,' Paul told an interviewer. 'It brought me every possible benefit. My acting improved and I achieved a greater control of myself . . . People should not be afraid of it,' he continued. 'Anything you can do to develop a realistic appraisal of yourself is immensely useful . . . Analysis is always interesting. You never stop learning. It's never really finished.'

Analysis helped Paul through a very difficult time. On the outside, nothing had changed. He was still frustrated at being 'owned' by a Hollywood studio which seemed to have entirely too much control over his life, especially where his finances and his integrity as an actor were concerned. His private life was still a mess. He and Jackie were having some difficult times and he hadn't seen Joanne for quite a while and missed her like crazy.

Yes, the same set of problems was still there, but Paul's way of looking at them had changed. He no longer felt powerless, guilt-ridden and overwhelmed. He took one day at a time and faced each problem as it cropped up instead of brooding and despairing. Analysing the way he really felt about things and why he felt that way helped Paul to deal with almost everything. He felt less helpless and therefore less depressed. His anxiety diminished, and with it his need to drink. From that point on, while Paul continued to enjoy his beers, he never felt the need to 'get drunk' and then act out his aggressive impulses.

Around this time, Paul did a film through Warner Bros. which he found interesting and enjoyed doing. Retitled *The Left-Handed Gun,* it was a film adaptation of Gore Vidal's TV play, *The Death of Billy the Kid.* Newman was glad of the chance to work with producer Fred Coe and director Arthur Penn, both of whom he'd worked with years earlier on TV. The film was revolutionary in that it portrayed Billy as a mixed up, misunderstood adolescent with basically good instincts rather than as an anti-social outlaw. *The Left-Handed Gun* opened to mixed reviews, but it has since become a cult classic, with Newman's performance praised as complex, subtle and powerful.

In 1982, almost a quarter century after it was made, Paul Newman gave *The Left-Handed Gun* his own personal appraisal in *Time* magazine: 'A little bit ahead of its time and a classic in Europe. To this day I still get $800 at the end of the year. Go to Paris right now, and I bet you it is playing in some tiny theatre,' Paul said, pleased that his work was still appreciated.

As an additional footnote, Gore Vidal and Newman had been friends ever since meeting soon after Paul arrived in Hollywood. To this day the Newmans, whom Vidal refers to as 'Miss Georgia and Mr Shaker Heights,' count him as one of their closest friends. All three are well-read, witty and liberal politically, and all three hate hypocrisy and man's inhumanity to man.

The fact that Gore is an inveterate bachelor and admitted bisexual, while the Newmans are family-oriented, never interfered with their friendship. Gore is a godfather to their firstborn daughter and a beloved uncle to the others.

Throwing himself into a project and enjoying it without the need for booze was a good experience for Paul. But soon something happened which was going to test his mettle and tax his newfound peace of mind: he and Joanne Woodward ran into each other by accident. Maybe it was because he was so much saner and calmer now; maybe it was because in some deep way analysis had made him realise she was the one; or maybe it was just because once they saw each other again, they couldn't resist. At any rate, Paul and Joanne resumed their love affair.

Again it seemed that Fate took a hand in deciding the affairs – and the affair – of Paul and Joanne. Just around the time they began to see each other again, 20th Century Fox, Joanne's studio, was looking for a handsome, magnetic actor to play the lead in their new film *The Long, Hot Summer,* to be produced by Jerry Wald. Fox decided Paul Newman would be perfect for the role of Ben Quick and had no trouble getting permission from Warner Bros., who was only too glad to rent out Newman for the customary fat fee. Paul's usual ire at being exploited was somewhat mitigated in this case when he found out who his female co-star would be.

Yes, it was Joanne Woodward. For the first time the lovers would work together in a movie, and naturally the prospect was exhilarating for both of them. One of the best parts about it was that the movie was to be shot on location in Clinton, Mississippi, a tiny backwater town not far from Jackson. They would be far away from Hollywood and its gossip mongers. For perhaps the first time in their relationship, they could enjoy the luxury of being together for days and weeks on end – and being together for a totally legitimate reason, too.

Joanne, being a 'Southern belle' by birth, was well prepared for the part, accent and all. But Paul, thorough as always in his role research, decided to immerse himself in the Mississippi culture beforehand. He travelled down to Clinton before the rest of the film people, and got a room. He spent the next few days hanging out in bars and poolrooms, mostly observing the native behaviour, watching how they moved and listening to them talk, absorbing their gestures and their attitudes. Paul's low-keyed manner, coupled with his ready grin and impressive physique (he was obviously no wimp), made a favourable impression on the 'good old boys.' The local folk readily accepted him, having no idea he was a famous movie star.

When the film crew arrived, the denizens of Clinton took Paul's movie star identity in stride. He remained popular with the townspeople throughout the shooting. In fact, some of the tougher ones among them proved their loyalty to Paul one night when they ejected a snooping Hollywood reporter from a bar, roughing him up and advising him to leave town post-haste.

This incident provided Newman with unconcealed satisfaction and glee. For years now reporters had dogged his and Joanne's every step, and the press had had a field day at their expense. Paul's exploits during his periods of heavy drinking had been sensationalised way beyond their importance, as had his image as an 'adulterer'. The harsh treatment given him by the press during these years left Newman with a bitterness that endures to this day. An intensely private person, he resents any intrusion into his personal life, by fans, neighbours or strangers of any kind – but especially the press.

He has given very few interviews over the years; those that he does give are usually in connection with his latest films. When he is interviewed, Paul uses the opportunity to discuss his political views (he's still a liberal after all these years), or his Newman's Own food business (whose profits go to a number of charitable causes). With his antic sense of humour, Paul may well derive enjoyment from the fact that, since his romance with Joanne and subsequent divorce from Jackie over 30 years ago, his life has not only been scandal-free, but highly altruistic and honourable. It's truly exemplary for a normal person, but especially for a celebrity.

Based on some short fictional works by William Faulkner, *The Long, Hot Summer* involves the romance between Ben Quick (Newman), a brash young redneck, and Clara Varner (Woodward), a sheltered, pampered girl from a rich family. Her father, Will Varner, a local tyrant used to getting his own way, hates Ben on sight and does his utmost to break up the romance, to no avail. The blustery Southern oligarch was played by Orson Welles, in his usual flamboyant style. This was Paul's first film with director Martin Ritt, with whom he was to share a rewarding, ongoing relationship.

The Long, Hot Summer is as sultry and steamy as its title suggests. Being thwarted lovers in real life, Paul and Joanne could identify with their characters on a gut level. There is a certain sexual tension that comes through on the screen and adds to the heavy, humid atmosphere of the film in an almost palpable way.

On screen, the pair play off each other very well. There's a magnetism and electricity that brings life and energy to their scenes together. A good example are the early scenes where the handsome young upstart, Ben Quick, brags in order to impress shy, innocent Clara – who is already impressed to the point of swooning just because of Ben's interest in her.

Finding that they worked well together on screen added yet another dimension to the already rich and varied relationship shared by Newman and Woodward. Creating something together through acting was especially fulfilling and exhilarating to them.

'For those times, *The Long, Hot Summer* was pretty hot stuff,' says a retired cameraman who was present at the filming. 'And if you think Paul and Joanne on the screen was hot stuff, you should have seen the footage I shot that later ended up on the cutting room floor because it was *too* hot!

'Never mind that,' he went on, his voyeuristic streak undiminished after all these years, 'that was nothing compared to what went on between them off the set. This was bona fide passion. Everyone knew they better not dare knock on the door of whichever trailer they were in at the time, or heads would roll. One guy who worked as a gofer swears that Newman once grabbed his boss (the assistant director) by the collar and said, as if he was real angry: 'If this trailer's rockin', don't bother knockin'! And don't you forget it, either.' Then Newman burst out laughing, but the guy's collar was really ripped. It was a joke but not a joke, if you know what I mean, and Newman was famous for those.'

During those hot days and nights in Mississippi, Paul and Joanne's commitment to each other was finalised. At this point they had no other option. Quite literally they felt as if they couldn't live without each other.

Of course, they still dreaded taking the final step that would inevitably cause hurt and unhappiness to Jackie and the children. As it happened, it was Jackie who saved Paul the trauma of filing for divorce. She filed on her own with a minimum of fuss, making no undue demands and causing few problems for her husband. It can't have been easy for Jackie, knowing that Paul and Joanne were together in Mississippi, doing love scenes both on the set and off. Even if she had accustomed herself to their affair, to the point where it wasn't quite so painful, Jackie had to live with the knowledge that soon the entire country would be able to see her erstwhile husband making love to his girlfriend on screen. It would have been hurtful to any woman, but Paul's celebrity made it worse.

In spite of this humiliating prospect, Jackie Witte remained a lady to the end, holding her head high and refraining from taking any kind of 'revenge' on Paul through the divorce. By giving in so gracefully, Jackie prevented the Newman divorce from becoming 'sensational' or 'scandalous' and thus made a difficult situation a littler easier for all three of them. Whether it was her own noble character or an unshakable love for Paul, Jackie made no waves.

Having Jackie file for divorce helped to diminish the burden of guilt Paul had been carrying. And even though there were regrets, it was a relief to have the situation settled relatively amicably after the long years of indecision and self-recrimination. It was a quiet, low-key time for Paul and Joanne as they remained in Hollywood, inseparable and finally living together, as they waited for the divorce to come through.

Finally it did, and after a love affair that had lasted on and off for five years, Paul Newman and Joanne Woodward became man and wife on January 29, 1958. Paul had turned 33 three days before the wedding, and Joanne would turn 28 in less than a month, so it was another special winter occasion for them to celebrate. Except that they were married at the Hotel El Rancho in Las Vegas, so it didn't *feel* like winter. It was a warm occasion in every way, shared by just a few close friends, and when it was over Paul and his radiant bride left for New York and a honeymoon in Great Britain.

They visited London first, staying at the famed Connaught Hotel, known then as 'one of the most civilised and unpretentious hotels in the world.' Not yet stars of international note, the Newmans were able to see the sights in England and visit pubs and restaurants without being hounded by paparazzi and fans. Like any honeymooners, they chose to spend most of their time alone, but they did look up a few friends, such as Peter Ustinov, the Ken Tynans, and Laurence Olivier.

From London, they moved on to Scotland, preferring to stay in small villages where they went for walks in the cold but not freezing weather, and frequented watering holes where they drank mugs of stout and spent hours talking to the local people.

Undoubtedly, Paul and Joanne's honeymoon had its passionate moments, but above all it was a time of serenity, a sweet oasis of peace after all the conflict and turmoil. For so long they had had to hide their love, like a secret gift which they dared not unwrap. Now at last the gift was theirs to open and examine and marvel over.

Even though he was happier than he'd been in years, Paul would take time to get over his divorce and to get used to his new marriage. It would also take time for him to forgive himself completely and be able to feel the joyfulness of being with Joanne.

'I feel guilty as hell about it, and I will carry that guilt for the rest of my life,' he said of the break-up of his first marriage.

And yet, it had to be, because there was a feeling inside him – a need – that would not be denied. 'Without her,' he says of Joanne Woodward, 'I'd be nowhere – nothing.'

Chapter 4

1958 was a banner year for Paul and Joanne. It started off with their marriage in January, their honeymoon in February, and then the beginning of their new life as a married couple. Deciding that Hollywood was a nice place to work but that they didn't want to live there, the Newmans rented an apartment in a graceful old building on the Upper East side of Manhattan. The place was large enough to accommodate Paul's three children when they came to visit, and the couple furnished it in a comfortable rather than lavish style. There were a few really fine pieces of furniture, however – such as a huge brass bed that once stood in a New Orleans brothel.

1958 showed every sign of being a banner year for the Newmans careerwise too. Being nominated for an Academy Award was an honour in itself for young Joanne Woodward, but actually winning the best actress Oscar for her role in *Three Faces of Eve* was recognition beyond even her wildest fantasies. The nine-year-old girl who vowed that she would become a great actress one day had actually realised that ambition at the age of 28.

Meantime, Paul Newman garnered his own honours that year. *The Long, Hot Summer* received good reviews in general, with Newman singled out for particular praise. For instance, *Time* magazine (evidently alluding to the down-home atmosphere of the film) called his performance 'keen as a crackle-edged scythe'.

Later, after a showing of *The Long, Hot Summer,* Paul
Newman was awarded the Cannes Film Festival Prize as Best
Actor of 1958. This honour was a harbinger of things to
come. For many years, the works of Paul Newman and
Joanne Woodward, either singly or together, would be
appreciated more in Europe (France especially) than in the
United States.

Paul's next film would earn him an Academy Award
nomination for best actor, the first of seven such nominations,
only the last of which he would win. The film was *Cat on a
Hot Tin Roof,* another Southern steamy drama based on the
classic play by Tennessee Williams. In it, Newman plays the
pivotal character, Brick, the young heir to a dynasty founded
by his dominating, bombastic and now dying father, 'Big
Daddy,' played superbly by Burl Ives. Brick, who is inwardly
tormented by the suicide of a close male friend of his, acts
sullen and withdrawn when he isn't outwardly hostile and
abusive to family members who make demands on him. He is
unable to deal with Big Daddy's fervent wish that he take over
as patriarch and head of the family – or the sexual desires of
his young wife, 'Maggie the Cat,' played by Elizabeth Taylor.

Elizabeth Taylor also received an Academy Award
nomination for *Cat on a Hot Tin Roof.* Although she didn't
win the Oscar, she received universal admiration for the
professionalism she displayed under the severe stress of losing
her husband, Mike Todd (the film's producer). His sudden
death in a plane crash came before the filming was complete.

Working with Elizabeth Taylor was memorable to Paul in
several ways. For one thing, he said of *Cat on a Hot Tin Roof,*
'That was the first of my pictures, except for the one I made
with Joanne, that I didn't have to carry pretty much on my
own. Before that, it had just worked out that I'd never played
with a star. In working with Elizabeth Taylor, I was
astonished to find that she was a real pro. She's not afraid to
take chances in front of people,' he went on. 'Usually, stars
become very protective of themselves and very self-indulgent,

but she's got a lot of guts. She'd go ahead and explore and risk falling on her face . . . not that she ever did.'

There was some criticism of writer-director Richard Brooks for eliminating the homosexual theme implicit in Williams's drama as well as some other Freudian elements from the film. For instance, in the original play, Brick's unwillingness to make love to his hot-blooded wife and thus ensure continuation of the family line, is because of his latent homosexuality and his grief at his male lover's suicide. In the film version, Brick is portrayed as a heavy drinker who is either too drunk or too depressed to make love to his wife.

In this film, as in *The Long, Hot Summer,* the steamy Southern heat is a metaphor for the repressed sexuality and explosive emotions of the characters. The tension builds as Maggie the Cat slinks around the bedroom in a slip, first teasing and seductive toward the handsome, shirtless Brick, then taunting and cruel as he rejects her once too often. Newman and Taylor performed excellently together, but their combined good looks and sex appeal alone would have been enough to send people rushing to the theatres to see this one. Despite its flaws scriptwise, *Cat on a Hot Tin Roof* was good for both their careers – as well as Metro-Goldwyn-Mayer, which once again had 'rented' Newman from Warner Bros.

Newman went on loan for his next picture as well, this time to Joanne's home studio, 20th Century Fox, which wanted to team them up again. For some unknown reason, Fox put Paul and Joanne in a comedy this time, even though neither of them had any kind of experience or track record in this genre. The film, *Rally 'Round the Flag, Boys,* was based on the Max Shulman novel of the same name. Described as 'a spoof on suburban living,' the thin plot revolves around a husband's (Paul Newman) problems with a flighty wife (Joanne Woodward) and a seductive neighbour (Joan Collins).

'I wasn't very good,' Paul acknowledges, 'but it was a good opportunity for me to try something new.' Even though

Paul's comedic talents in *Rally 'Round the Flag Boys* were limited, he and Joanne were good drawing cards just by virtue of it being the first film they made together since their marriage. The film made money for Fox, thanks to a public that was in the mood for mindless frothy entertainment.

Paul's next film, *The Young Philadelphians,* was the first he had made with Warner Bros. in quite some time – and it would turn out to be the last. Paul, who was on the verge of buying out his contract, wasn't too thrilled with the film and agreed to make it on the condition that Warners would release him to appear on Broadway early in 1959 in Tennessee Williams's *Sweet Bird of Youth* with Geraldine Page. *The Young Philadelphians* was based on a novel by Richard Powell about a sharp young lawyer on his way up the ladder of success.

Fast-paced, slick and sophisticated, and with a talented cast which also included Barbara Rush, Alexis Smith, Billie Burke, Brian Keith and Robert Vaughn, the film was a commercial success. It turned out to be a better film, and a better role for Paul Newman that he had anticipated.

According to Lawrence J Quick, author of *The Films of Paul Newman, The Young Philadephians* ' ... attractively showcased Newman in one of the roles with which he was to become strongly identified, the sleek, slick young man on the make for success and women, who always seemed to land on his feet like a cat and waded through all obstacles with brazen insouciance.'

At this point, Paul Newman felt confident enough to take a gamble on the success of his own future career. In a brave show of independence, he made a deal to buy his contract from Warner Bros. for $500,000, an astounding amount of money back then.

For a long time Newman had resented being 'owned' by Warners and being forced to appear in any film they chose for him – even at other studios, to which Warners 'lent' him at a handsome profit. For instance, for the last film he did with

Warner Bros., Newman received $17,500 while for years Warners had been receiving $75,000 each time they loaned him out.

In buying out his contract, Newman was following in the footsteps of actors like Kirk Douglas, whom Paul had met some years earlier and with whom he maintains a friendship to this day. From the start of his career, Kirk had insisted on one-picture contracts. The only time he had deviated from this rule was when he signed a contract with Warners for several films, the first of which, *Champion,* made him a star. To obtain his release from the contract, Douglas agreed to make a film for Warner Bros. for nothing.

'I had to pay half a million dollars for my freedom,' Paul said, 'but it was worth it. If I hadn't done it, I would soon have had ulcers.'

The deal turned out to be well worth it to Paul financially, too. Thanks to three top-grossing movies he would make in the next three years – *Exodus, The Hustler,* and *Sweet Bird of Youth* – his debt was taken care of in as much time.

Making a specific deal for each film with whatever studio was backing it worked to Paul's advantage. Once he paid off his debt to Warner Bros., his income increased dramatically. 'I made $17,000 for my work in *Cat on a Hot Tin Roof,'* he said. 'Three years later, for the picture *Sweet Bird of Youth,* I got a $350,000 guarantee, with a chance to make more if the picture did very well.'

In the beginning of 1959 Paul was more than happy to leave Hollywood behind and return to the New York stage. It was an honour for him to play opposite the brilliantly talented Geraldine Page in a production of *Sweet Bird of Youth,* directed by the venerable Elia Kazan. Page was in the role of Alexandra del Lago, a fading film star, and Newman played her live-in gigolo, Chance Wayne. Since the character of a pay-for-play beach boy wasn't an easy one for Paul to identify with, *Sweet Bird of Youth* presented a real challenge for him.

'We took three weeks to rehearse the Broadway

production,' Newman recalled. 'For the most part, I relied on the director, Elia Kazan, for what I did. He has broad shoulders. His invention, imagination, and patience are extraordinary. He helped me see that I had four things to comment on in portraying the character of Chance Wayne: the beauty of the relationship between men and women; the social disaster of a family that has lost the esteem of others; the fetish of youth and the importance of the fetish in our country; and the loving remembrance of youth. That was a lot,' Paul continued, 'but there were areas of Chance Wayne I never really got, including the aspect of the male whore, so it was always interesting to see what I could do with him.'

Paul definitely had the looks for the part, and with the help of Elia Kazan's coaching, he was able to play Chance Wayne convincingly. The play was a huge success, both with the critics and the public, with Newman's performances receiving praise, along with the performances of Geraldine Page and the other cast members, Sidney Blackmer, Rip Torn, Madeleine Sherwood, Diana Hyland and Bruce Dern.

Appearing nightly with such a distinguished group was exciting for Paul, but in time the pressure of being in a hit Broadway show began to take its toll. The following quotation, as reported by Lillian and Helen Ross in their publication, *The Player,* is a good description of what it's like for almost any performer to appear in a long-running stage show.

'After ten months . . . on Broadway, it got so that going to the theatre each night was like facing the dentist,' Paul admitted. 'I'd try to get to the theatre early, so I'd have my dinner at five o'clock. Before every performance, I'd drink a couple of jiggers of honey for energy and for my throat; I'd lose three pounds by the end of every performance. I'd sack out from about seven to five minutes to eight. Then I'd sit in the shower at the theatre and collect my wits.

'As I was going to the theatre for my last performance in the play,' Paul recalled, 'I thought, I feel utterly exhausted. And all of a sudden, I started bawling like a baby. I thought, I'll never say these words again. I'll never have this specific laugh again. I'll never have this kind of quiet near the end of the third act. Never this specific quiet.'

While Paul was busy with *The Young Philadelphians* and then *Sweet Bird of Youth* on Broadway, Joanne was busy with her own film commitments. Unfortunately, nothing she was offered around this time came anywhere near *Three Faces of Eve* in scope or quality. Joanne turned in her usual excellent acting job in each of the films made around this time, but none turned out to be a finished product of which she could feel truly proud.

The Sound and the Fury, very loosely based on Faulkner's novel of the same name, was little more than a hodge-podge, with the character which Joanne played being described by one reviewer as a 'Southern simpleton'. Somewhat more enjoyable to Joanne was her role in *The Stripper,* because it afforded her the opportunity to be 'sexy and voluptuous' on screen.

Yet another disastrous film made after *Eve* was *The Fugitive Kind,* released in 1960, in which Joanne Woodward starred with Anna Magnani and Marlon Brando.

'I hated it,' Joanne said of the movie years later, 'though I loved Anna Magnani. That beautiful woman ... she was very kind to me, very gentle in her own strange way. Let's see, Anna was my age (42) when we made the film, maybe a few years older, and very ambivalent about her looks. She'd tell the cameraman she wanted every line in her face to show on film, yet she was very vain and it was touching − she hid her neck with scarves and was constantly pushing them closer to her chinline. As you get older and the wrinkles come, you realise the tragedy of the worship of the young in films.'

At the time, Joanne was in her late twenties and at the peak of her own beauty. She didn't have to worry about wrinkles or camera angles, any more than Anna Magnani had at her age.

For her next film, Joanne was teamed up again with her husband. For whatever reasons, the only successful films Joanne had been in after *Three Faces of Eve* were those she made with Paul. The reason had nothing to do with Joanne per se. No one could doubt her acting skill or her appeal to the public. It was most likely because the films she appeared in singly after *Eve* were seriously flawed and did not possess mass appeal. By this time Newman and Woodward were tremendously popular as a couple, similar to Spencer Tracy and Katherine Hepburn or Bogart and Bacall. And their next film, *From the Terrace,* proved that the Newman's combined popularity was more important than good reviews in determining box office success.

Fortunately, *From the Terrace* was shot in New York, so that Paul, who was still appearing in *Sweet Bird of Youth,* could film it by day while performing in the play at night. It was a rough schedule, but the fact that he was working with his wife made moonlighting worthwhile for Paul.

'I've made three movies with Joanne . . . and we find we like working together,' Paul said around this time. 'We respect each other tremendously, and if one of us criticises the other, the criticism is taken as gospel. When we do a scene together, we both know we can't rely on tricks, and if one of us tries to, the other is sure to sound off about it. You have to be married to have that kind of freedom,' Paul finished, flashing his famous grin.

Losely based on John O'Hara's best-selling novel, 20th Century-Fox's version of *From the Terrace* featured Paul Newman as Alfred Eaton, another young man on an upwardly mobile path. Eventually tiring of the rat race, he leaves his ambitious wife (Joanne Woodward) for a simple, undemanding type (Ina Balin) whom he feels loves him for himself rather than his earning potential.

Although the critics came down on *From the Terrace* for being 'flimsy and poorly motivated' and a travesty of O'Hara's novel, the public went to see it anyway, and the picture made money. Even today, Paul and Joanne retain a certain fondness for the film also. Newman called it 'Pretty good soap opera,' and Woodward said, 'I love the way I looked in it – like Lana Turner.'

Newman started filming *From the Terrace* while still appearing in his Broadway show, but by the end of the film Joanne was the one who was moonlighting – as a mom-to-be! Paul and Joanne's first child, Eleanor Theresa, was born late in 1959. A beautiful blonde girl, she has been called Nell from the start.

Today when a married actress has a baby, it has little or no effect on the course of her career – that is, unless the actress herself opts for a hiatus. There is usually no outside pressure and probably no pressure from her husband or family to stop working. But things were different in 1959. Even before having the baby, Joanne had willingly decided to put her marriage before her career, and Paul's career before her own. Now that she was a mother as well as a wife, Joanne's career was, of her own accord, even less important.

One thing Joanne knew she was not going to do was sit home with the baby while Paul went away on location. She had seen first-hand what an arrangement like that could do to a marriage. So, early in 1960, Joanne packed up baby Nell and left with Paul for Israel, where he was to star in *Exodus* for United Artists.

Joanne enjoyed being at her husband's side in an exotic and beautiful location. Some members of the impressive cast, which included Eva Marie Saint, Ralph Richardson, Peter Lawford, Lee J Cobb, Sal Mineo, John Derek and Jill Haworth, were already known to Joanne, and she and Paul quickly made friends with the others.

Exodus, based on the best-selling novel by Leon Uris, concerned the founding of the State of Israel in 1947. In it, Newman was to play the role of Ari Ben Canaan, who masterminds the escape of more than 600 Jewish refugees from Cyprus and into Palestine. The character faces a personal crisis when he falls in love with an American nurse and befriends an Arab.

Being of Jewish heritage himself, Paul Newman was thrilled with the opportunity of being in the film. He spent some time getting to know the country and its people as he prepared for his role. Everything was fine – until actual filming started. At that time, Newman and other cast members had problems with its talented but often temperamental director, Otto Preminger. Great as he was in some respects, Preminger was also dictatorial and arbitrary, often provocative in his decisions. Although skilful in dealing with crowd and action scenes, Preminger was not tolerant or receptive to actors' opinions. This rubbed Paul the wrong way, since he was accustomed to directors allowing him to make script changes and alterations in his role if he felt they were necessary artistically. He was used to having responsible input in his films.

The conflicts that plagued the production of *Exodus* affected the finished film adversely. It was panned by the critics, who called Newman's performance 'stiff' and 'lacking in depth and emotion.' Ironically, *Exodus* grossed more at the box office than any of Newman's other movies, and he ended up making almost $200,000 for a film that actually hurt his career rather than helped it.

But, if Paul was one down with *Exodus*, the next film on his agenda more than compensated for this setback. That film was *The Hustler*, which many people think is one of the best American films ever made. It offers much on many levels, not only being a compelling story, but also a film with many levels of meaning.

On the most basic level, *The Hustler* is a tale about a brash young pool shark, 'Fast Eddie' Felson, played by Newman. He travels around the country with his manager/sidekick Charlie (Myron McCormick), hustling pool games for a living. He pretends to be a drunken novice, letting his opponents defeat him a few times and win his money before he displays his true prowess, taking his dumbfounded victims for all they've got.

After months of insignificant wins in small town pool halls, Eddie decides he's ready for the big time, and he and Charlie arrive in New York. There Eddie puts out word that he wants to take on the best pool shooter in the country, Minnesota Fats, superbly played by Jackie Gleason. Their eventual match runs for hours on end, and Fast Eddie is the winner all the way – until his overconfident attitude and over drinking make him blow it.

Broke and disillusioned, he picks up a girl in an all-night restaurant. Sarah (hauntingly played by Piper Laurie) goes homes with Eddie for the sake of the bottle of booze which he buys, but she's not a cheap floozie. She's a sensitive and vulnerable, but embittered girl, shattered by her crippled leg and her damaged life, and she seeks to drown her loneliness and pain in alcohol.

Eddie moves in with Sarah and drifts around town, hustling games in third-rate pool halls. One night he defeats a player who gets wise to his hustle, and the loser and his pals jump Eddie in an alley, breaking both his thumbs.

During this time, when he is helpless and hurt, Sarah tenderly nurses him back to health, and love blossoms between them. Her love for Eddie makes Sarah whole again. She stops drinking and begins to hope that the two of them can live a normal life together. She begs Eddie to give up hustling and get a real job.

Eddie wants to be with Sarah, too – but he says that first he wants to make a pile of money playing pool, and *then* they can settle down. He gets involved with Bert Gordon (George C Scott), a ruthless stake-horse with loads of money. Bert wants to back Eddie, arranging high-stake games for him – in return for a 70 percent cut.

Sarah is against this partnership, knowing that Eddie can't really 'win' if he's in league with Bert, who is the personification of greed and evil. In turn, Bert hates Sarah, because he knows that in spite of her vulnerability, she may have the power to take Eddie away from him before he can completely exploit his pool-playing talents.

The ill-fated trio set off for Kentucky, where Bert wants to set Eddie up with a millionaire billiards addict. They go to the millionaire's mansion, and Newman is spirited downstairs by Bert. Alone among rich strangers, Sarah gets drunk and then hysterical. She goes back to the hotel where Bert later joins her.

Meantime, Eddie is left to play billiards, a variation of pool which he isn't even familiar with. He quickly masters the game and defeats the millionaire. At the same time, he realises that Sarah is right – hustling is no good and he resolves to stop it as of then. He refuses to ride back to the hotel with Bert, preferring to walk all the way back and clear his mind.

Panicky at the idea of losing his protégé and meal ticket, Bert rushes back to the hotel, where he tells Sarah that Eddie never cared for her to begin with and is planning to dump her. Sarah is already drunk, and Gordon undermines her fragile psyche to the extent that she goes back to the room she shares with Eddie and kills herself, thinking all the way to the end that Eddie has betrayed her even as he is on his way back to tell her that his hustling days are over and he wants to be with her.

The forces of good jousting against the forces of evil, the power of love pitted against the power of greed, alienation and the possibility of redemption – these are the greater themes of *The Hustler*, which some reviewers describe as a modern Greek tragedy.

That a black and white film made in 1961 with a small cast and a relatively low budget could be 'an interesting story about pool hustlers' and at the same time invite comparison to Greek tragedy is a kind of screen 'miracle' that had many contributing factors.

First and foremost, credit was due to Robert Rossen, who

not only produced and directed the film, but also, with Sidney Carroll, wrote the screenplay based on the novel *The Hustler* by Walter Tevis.

The film also delivers incredible visual impact. As the reviewer in *Time* magazine said: 'Cameraman Gene Shufton has artfully preserved what actor Gleason calls 'the dirty, antiseptic look of poolrooms' – spots on the floor, toilets stuffed up, but the tables brushed immaculately, like green jewels lying in the mud . . . '

The Hustler was a rare example of what can happen when all the elements of a film come together, creating a work that is truly greater than the sum of its parts. As Paul V Beckley in the *New York Herald Tribune* put it: 'The writing, the directing, and the acting all have that kind of intense unanimity that convinces you everyone involved understood and felt what they were concerned with.'

Virtually the entire cast of *The Hustler* was excellent, with George C Scott and Jackie Gleason receiving special recognition. But soaring above all of the other factors who contributed to the film's greatness were Paul Newman and Piper Laurie. Playing two lost souls at cross purposes, yet needing each other desperately, they delivered poignantly real and emotionally unforgettable performances.

As Alton Cook wrote in his review in the *New York World Telegram and Sun:* 'Paul Newman is always a dominant figure in any scene, but there is something extra this time in his intense ardour as the man who treats a game with religious zeal that at times mounts to mania. His standard is high, but he has surpassed it this time.'

Newman himself gave an interesting slant on the strength of his performance in *The Hustler* when he spoke to an interviewer about his early films: 'The character of the young lawyer that I played in *The Young Philadelphians* was much closer to me as a human being – and much duller – than Eddie Felson, the character I played in *The Hustler*. But the characters that are farthest away from my own personality are the ones I feel most successful with,' Paul confided. 'The farther away from me a character is, the more I find there is to dig into.'

The film received nine Academy Award nominations, including one for Paul as best actor of 1961. Newman lost for the second time, with the award going instead to an actor who was born not in America but Germany, Maximillian Schell, for his performance in *Judgement at Nuremberg*. Ironically Newman won the British Academy Award as best actor of that year.

In a rare moment of candour, the usually circumspect Paul Newman told *Playboy* magazine about how he felt at losing the Oscar for the second time – and how his wife Joanne helped him through a bad night.

'I remember we were staying there (at their home in Beverly Hills) right after I lost the Academy Award for the *The Hustler,*' Paul said. 'I was really hurt by that one. I thought old Fast Eddie was a fairly original character. Anyway, being the perfect therapist, Joanne dragged me out by the hand to the garage. We had a little hideaway out there really away from the family. She said, 'We're going to take a little caviar and a little champagne out there and watch a very bad show on television.' Well,' Paul admitted, 'we never got around to the show.'

Ironically, Paul Newman *would* win a best actor Oscar for his role as Fast Eddie Felson, but not until 25 years later when Hollywood finally gave him this long-over-due Oscar for *The Color of Money*. This competent but inferior sequel to *The Hustler* was lacking in both emotional intensity and believability, but it received a big media-hype and enjoyed a popular success which was most likely due to its popular young sex symbol star, Tom Cruise, and its popular older sex symbol star, Paul Newman.

Although Paul Newman's performance in *The Color of Money* was no better than his performance in the other six films for which he'd been nominated as best actor, only to lose, such are the vagaries of Hollywood Oscars. So, when he finally won in 1986 for *The Color of Money,* can anyone wonder why Paul wasn't there to receive his Oscar in person?

Chapter 5

After his hard work and eventual triumph in *The Hustler,* Newman was offered a film deal which he just couldn't turn down. Making a proposed movie called *Paris Blues* with United Artists would mean having his wife as co-star, and their pal Martin Ritt as director. Ever since doing *The Long, Hot Summer,* Newman and Ritt had looked forward to working together again. An added incentive was that the film was to be shot on location in Paris.

On the surface, the plot of the film – that of two American jazz musicians, one black and one white, trying to make it in Paris – was off-beat enough to be interesting to Newman, especially since the film would feature music composed by Duke Ellington and played by Louis Armstrong. Newman felt the interracial theme was timely and thought that he and Sidney Poitier as the jazz players and Joanne Woodward and Diahann Carroll as their girlfriends made for a promising cast.

The only problem – and it was a big one – was with the script. Too many writers had done too many revisions, and the end result was a plot that lacked cohesion, and characters that were little more than cardboard cut-outs.

The critics were quick to pick up on these failings, and even the excellent musical score of the film and its four talented co-stars weren't enough to save it. 'The characters are no more than attitudes, so it is by no means the fault of Miss

Woodward, Miss Carroll, Newman or Poitier that they come off so poorly,' Beckley wrote in the *New York Herald Tribune*.

Even so, all concerned with the film had good intentions, and both Paul and Joanne retain their good feelings about it to this day. 'I had some fun with that one,' Paul told *Time* magazine, 'not that it is a great film.' And Joanne called *Paris Blues* 'a strange and interesting film that was ahead of its time.'

Even if *Paris Blues* flopped, a Newman-Woodward collaboration that came about later in 1961 was a rousing success – the birth of their second daughter, Melissa Stewart, nicknamed Lissie. Her middle name was in honour of the Newman's dear friend, screenwriter Stewart Stern.

Whereas many, if not most show business marriages would have felt the strain of both husband and wife appearing in several films while also producing two babies in only three years, Paul and Joanne were blissfully happy. That obviously attested to their loving bond.

Their lifestyle wasn't lavish, especially by Hollywood standards. But it suited the Newmans perfectly. 'I can live very comfortably on my earnings,' Paul said around that time, 'but I don't have much in the way of material possessions beyond the furniture in our New York apartment, a few paintings, a Volkswagen, and a Lambretta motor scooter, which I use for getting around the city . . . We go out to Hollywood to live whenever Joanne or I have to work there, but . . . what we want is a place up in Connecticut where we can go in the summertime . . .'

Because Paul's ex-wife Jackie had remarried and moved with the kids to California, the Newmans decided it would be more practical to buy a house out there. They used their Beverly Hills home whenever a film commitment came up, having Scott, Susie and Stephanie stay with them whenever their school schedules would permit.

Before long, the Newmans' dream of owning property and a home in Connecticut finally came true. Paul had fallen in love with the New England countryside while attending Yale Drama School, and Connecticut made sense because it wasn't far from New York. The piece of property which they eventually purchased was in Westport, a picturesque seaside town within easy commuting distance from Manhattan. At that time Westport was quite rural, and the eleven acres the Newmans purchased contained not only an apple orchard, but a part of the Aspetuck River which still contained trout and was deep enough for boating. Besides the house, the property also included a barn dating back to the 1780's, which Paul and Joanne remodelled and eventually turned into a guesthouse and screening room.

They named their new home Nook House. As Paul explained, 'When we bought the house and we came back to Los Angeles, I hadn't seen the older kids for a while. We were describing the place to them . . . We'd been trying to think of a name for it. Susie, who at that time must have been nine, said, "Well, it sounds like it's got a lot of nooks and crannies in it. Why don't you call it Nook House?" I said, 'Nook House it is.'

Their rustic home in Westport has always been Paul and Joanne's preferred place of residence. They cultivated friendships with a few of the locals, but by and large the Newmans kept to themselves. Their growing family, which now included Nell, Lissie – and Scott, Susan and Stephanie part of the time – was enough for Paul and Joanne, along with certain close and favoured friends who would come for visits.

With his growing family, the Connecticut property, a home in Beverly Hills, and the apartment in New York, Paul needed to work steadily. In spite of the failure of *Paris Blues,* he was still considered a big box office draw and was constantly besieged with film offers. In 1962, Newman jumped at the chance to reprise his role of Chance Wayne in the movie version of *Sweet Bird of Youth.* Again his leading lady was Geraldine Page, in the role of the ageing film star who seeks to forget her fading beauty by distracting herself with alcohol, hashish and keeping pretty young men.

Both Page and Newman received good reviews. However, Richard Brooks, who had also directed the film version of *Cat on a Hot Tin Roof,* was again lambasted by the critics for 'watering down' Tennessee Williams's flagrant sexual and moral themes in deference to the stultified 'sweetness and light and happy endings' attitude promulgated by Hollywood studio heads.

Newman had long disliked the studio system and its short-sighted, limited artistic standards. In an attempt to have more financial independence, and be able to control his projects as an actor, Paul teamed up with his friend and colleague, director Martin Ritt, to form a production company.

'It's called Jodell Productions, after the first syllable of Joanne's name and the second syllable of Ritt's wife's name,' Paul reported enthusiastically.

Their first joint venture was a 1962 film called *Adventures of a Young Man,* based on a short story by Ernest Hemmingway. It was only a cameo appearance for Newman, as he reprised his TV role as *The Battler,* but he felt the role – and the film – were worthwhile artistically. His instinct proved correct in terms of the critics, who praised his performance as the punch-drunk old fighter. This role was especially memorable, because with his elaborate – and difficult to apply – make-up, the handsome Paul Newman was unrecognisable.

The next film Newman and Ritt made as partners was to prove their most successful collaboration ever. The film was *Hud,* in which Paul played the role of Hud Bannon, a surly, selfish Texas cattle rancher. Good-looking and hard-drinking, he is both a man's man and a ladies' man, used to getting his own way. He has no deep-seated emotions, and explains his deadness of soul with, 'My mother loved me, but she died.' Hud is trying to have his father declared senile so that he can sell the family ranch to oilmen.

Newman spent his usual amount of time researching the role. He went to Texas and actually worked on a cattle ranch, doing all the jobs that Hud Bannon would have done. By the time filming began, Paul's hands were calloused, his skin was deeply tanned, and he walked and talked like a cowboy.

But Paul's real challenge came in trying to capture the essence of Hud, a character who was attractive on the outside but rotten to the core. Newman got upset when some reviewers said he was 'too handsome' for the role and his good looks made Hud less believable as a 'bad guy.'

To Newman, these reviewers missed the whole point of his performance, and this upset him greatly. 'To me, *Hud* made the simple statement that people sometimes grow up at tragic expense to other people,' Paul said in a *Playboy* interview. 'I tried to give Hud all the superficial external graces, including the right swing of the body. I took out as many wrinkles as possible. I indicated that he boozed very well, was great with the broads, had a lot of guts, was extraordinarily competent at his job, but had a single tragic flaw: He didn't give a goddam what happened to anyone else. That tragic flaw simply went over everybody's head − especially the reviewers' − and he became a kind of antihero, especially among teenagers,' Paul lamented.

But Newman could comfort himself with the fact that at least some reviewers' perceptions of *Hud* were accurate. For instance, Bosley Crowther wrote in the *New York Times:* 'The sureness and integrity of it (*Hud*) are as crystal clear as the plot is spare . . . with a fine cast of performers, he (Martin Ritt) has people who behave and talk so truly that it is hard to shake them out of your mind. Paul Newman is tremendous − a potent, voracious man, restless with all his crude ambitions, arrogant with his contempt, and churned up inside with all the meanness and misgivings of himself.'

Despite some misconceptions, *Hud* was a huge success, not only with the critics but with the public. It received seven

Academy Award nominations, including one for Paul Newman as best actor and one for Patricia Neal for her role as the housekeeper who is attracted to Hud but knows what he really is and manages to resist him. Patricia Neal won the Oscar for the best actress of 1963. For the third time in a row, Paul Newman lost.

Rumours began to circulate that Newman's losses were 'political' in nature. Because of his supposed feuds with Jack Warner and because he bought his way out of his Warner Bros. contract, Newman was perceived as being a malcontent and a rebel. Moreover, by openly condemning Hollywood's values and choosing to live with his family in Connecticut, Paul was thought to be not only a loner, but a snob. He had thumbed his nose at Hollywood, it was felt, and nominating him three times and letting him lose three times was believed by many to be Hollywood's way of thumbing its nose back at him.

Just as the excellence of *The Hustler* was followed by the inane box office flop, *Paris Blues,* Newman followed his smash hit *Hud* with a mindless comedy called *A New Kind of Love.* This picture also concerned Americans in Paris, but this time their adventures were of the amorous variety. A playboy-type newspaper columnist, Steve Sherman (Newman) is exiled to Paris after being caught with his publisher's wife. On the plane trip over he meets Samantha Blake (Woodward) a dowdy, almost mannish career woman. A mover and shaker in ladies' fashions for a major store chain, she's on a buying trip to Paris.

Initially, Steve and Samantha are turned off by each other. He finds her cold and unattractive and she finds him boorish and arrogant. But at a St Catherine's Day celebration (where single girls pray for husbands) Samantha has a vision of St Catherine who tells her to jazz up her appearance and let the passionate woman inside her come out. She does the whole bit with her hair, make-up, clothes – and even acquires a sexy, teasing manner with men.

She meets up with Steve, who doesn't recognise her, and takes her for a glamorous, high-priced call girl. Samantha plays up this impression by making up wild lies about her life as the 'Sultana of Sin'. Steve writes a column about her doings, which is a big hit, and they fall in love. By then Steve doesn't mind that Samantha and Sultana are one and the same.

Produced, directed, and written by Melville Shavelson, *A New Kind of Love* was filled with sight gags, snappy quips and camera tricks galore. But none of this was enough to turn it into a good film. The plot was weak, the characters were one-dimensional, and Paul Newman and Joanne Woodward were not right for the lead roles.

Judith Crist in her *New York Herald Tribune* review describes the pretentious and trendy 'pow-bam-sock-wow' opening of the film, which she says '. . . provides immediate stupefaction − and sets the tone for the ensuing banalities . . . juvenile sex play and sophomoric camera tricks that go on for nigh to two unsolid hours.' Referring to Newman and Woodward, she says that '. . . those two usually distinguished performers are entitled to a fling − but Doris Day and Rock Hudson they're not − and shouldn't aspire to be.'

Joanne herself disagrees. '*A New Kind of Love* was just not a very good film,' she said. 'I don't think it has to do with Paul and me and the chemistry or lack of it.'

Later, in referring to *A New Kind of Love*, Paul blamed his wife for the fiasco, but in an affectionately teasing way: 'Joanne read it (the script) and said, "Hey, this would be fun to do together. Read it." I read it and said, "Joanne, it's just a bunch of one-liners." And she said, "You son of a bitch. I've been carting your children around, taking care of them at the expense of my career, taking care of you and your house." And I said, "That is what I said. It's a terrific script. I can't think of anything I'd rather do." This is what is known as a reciprocal trade agreement,' he finished, grinning good-naturedly.

Joanne Woodward couldn't seem to get a winning film to save her life during this time. Even though she was busy with two young daughters, as well as Paul's children from his previous marriage, and even though she had decided from the beginning that Paul's career should come first, it must have been discouraging for her when the few films she did appear in were box office disasters.

Signpost to Murder, the only film she'd done without Paul in years, was yet another disappointment. 'Oh, my heart,' she said, clutching her chest when an interviewer asked about the movie, 'what I remember most about that one is that we were shooting the film the day John Kennedy died. We had an awful director and the last scene was so bad we decided to throw it out and improvise on camera. I think the movie ran 45 minutes,' Joanne continued sardonically, 'but I liked the way I looked in the main opening shot. I was wearing a bathing suit, a large hat, and high heels.'

Paul's next picture, also made in 1963, didn't fare much better. Called *The Prize,* it was an ill-conceived mixture of adventure and romance, with some comedy thrown in. In it, Newman plays another hard-drinking womaniser, this time a Nobel prize-winning novelist. While in Stockholm to receive the prize, another winner, a physicist and friend of Newman's character, is kidnapped, and he sets out to find the missing man.

The film was dismissed by the critics, who thought the plot thin and lacking in motivation. Again, Newman was criticised for his failings as a comic actor. Certain scenes in *The Prize* – such as one in which Newman finds himself in a nudist camp – called for the debonair touch of a Cary Grant or a David Niven, which Newman couldn't deliver.

Despite the film's shortcomings, Newman enjoyed working again with director Mark Robson, who had directed *From the Terrace,* as well as with the competent cast which included Edward G Robinson, Elke Sommer, and Diane Baker.

'I had more fun making *The Prize* than any picture I've

made (so far),' Newman said. 'I mean just fun – running into the studio in the morning, filled with all kinds of inventions . . . that was great fun for me to do.'

Undaunted by his previous lack of success with screen comedies, Paul essayed the genre again in his next film. *What a Way to Go*, in 1964. Shirley MacLaine played the lead in this farce about a millionairess who loses one husband after another in bizarre accidents and wacky situations. Newman plays the second of her five husbands, a painter living in Paris (again!) who invents a machine that changes music in to paintings. After achieving fortune and fame through this strange gadget, he eventually falls into the machine and is killed.

Even with an impressive cast which included Robert Mitchum, Dean Martin, Gene Kelly, Bob Cummings, Dick Van Dyke and Margaret Dumont as well as Newman, the film didn't take off as expected. Paul, however, got some encouraging reviews from the critics, who felt that his comedic skills were improving. Besides, his role in *What a Way to Go* was only a minor one.

At this point, Paul Newman interrupted his film career to return to the New York stage – this time in the company of his wife. The play, *Baby Want a Kiss,* by James Costigan, was presented off-Broadway, under the auspices of The Actors Studio, to which the play's proceeds would go. In it, Paul and Joanne portray a married couple who are famous movie stars, but there any resemblance to their real personalities ends. The couple in the play are revealed through a visit to a writer friend of theirs who has not achieved their success. The playwright himself, James Costigan, plays their friend, and the ony other cast member besides the Newmans and Costigan is a sheep dog. During the visit to their old friend, the glamorous movie stars reveal themselves as being phony, sex-hungry, publicity-mad, and self-serving. They seem to bear no similarity to the couple the writer once knew.

Baby Want a Kiss is essentially a slick and sophisticated

comedy, and Newman received his best review in this genre yet. It was said that the excellent direction of Frank Corsaro was in large part responsible for Newman's improvement, but this turned out to be beside the point, because the play itself was not well-received by the public. This was a disappointment to the Newman's, not so much for their own sake, but for the sake of their beloved Actors Studio, which they wanted to see benefit as much as possible from the production.

Newman's next film project was a very ambitious one, taken on by Paul and his production company partner Martin Ritt. The 1964 film was entitled *The Outrage* and based on the Japanese film *Rashomon* by Akira Kurosawa, and the stage play by the same name. In the original story, two 19th century Europeans travelling in Japan are accosted, with the husband being murdered and his wife raped. The point of *Rashomon* is that the same sequence of events is told from several different viewpoints by several different people, and it is left up to the viewer or reader to determine the truth, if indeed there is such a thing.

Ritt and screenplay writer Michael Kanin decided to move the *Rashomon* story to contemporary America, with Laurence Harvey and Claire Bloom, as the man and wife who fall victim to violence and Paul Newman as the Mexican bandit who is their attacker.

From the start, Paul thought of this role as one of the greatest challenges of his career. As Newman said of his character, 'He was an absolute primitive, which I had never played, with an entirely different sense of movement and an accent I was not familiar with . . . I did it because I didn't think I could do it,' he added.

To prepare for his role in *The Outrage* Paul went down to Mexico on his own and hung out with the locals. 'I lived down there for two weeks,' he said. 'I literally lifted the accent from a young boy who'd been to Detroit, learned to speak English and come back. I got about 2,000 feet of tape of him telling stories and what have you,' Paul went on, admitting that he also 'stole the voice from a man whose father fought with Zapata, a marvellous guy, a bell-hop in a hotel ... you could hardly understand what he was saying ... I had two weeks of rehearsal in which to try and incorporate all of that ... the gestures are so different there (in Mexico). There are no big, broad Latin gestures or anything.'

Years later, Newman was still insisting that in terms of acting, '*The Outrage* is my best work, if I have to look at it for the work. I don't know if it is my best movie – that you've got to separate. I can only look at it and speculate, really,' he continued, 'but I hope that there is no residual element of anything that I have done before that is in the picture.'

What Paul meant was that in his portrayal of the Mexican bandit in *The Outrage,* he felt that he had started from scratch, with nothing in his previous career or personal life to draw upon. In terms of his voice, his accent, his gestures and expressions, he had to take on another personality. And in that he was able to accomplish such a thing, Paul felt proud of himself as an actor.

Unfortunately, Newman also felt that his own efforts and everyone else's went largely unnoticed and unappreciated because, as he put it, *The Outrage* was 'a picture that never got any attention or real circulation at all.'

Paul's next film, which went into production early in 1965, was one of those hodge-podge conglomerations which Newman should have known enough to stay away from. *Lady L,* adapted from the Romain Gary novel of the same name, was described as a 'comedy adventure drama', and it took place in Paris – the scene of many of Newman's most disastrous films. On the up side, the film was to be directed by Peter Ustinov, a talented and colourful character in his own right, and just the sort of person Newman most enjoyed working with. As a further incentive, Paul's female co-star was to be Sophia Loren.

Still, a synopsis of the plot of *Lady L* should have been

enough to warn an experienced actor that another box office flop was in store. The action takes place in Paris in 1905 and concerns the adventures of Armand (Newman), an anarchist and French-style Robin Hood who steals from the rich and gives to the poor. He falls in love with Louise (Sophia Loren), a beautiful, impoverished laundress who ends up marrying a British nobleman, Lord Lendale (played by David Niven). This marriage notwithstanding, Armand and Louise remain lovers for the next 50 years.

In this far-fetched scenario, David Niven had a definite advantage; at least he and the character he played were of the same nationality. Loren, an Italian, and Newman, an American, cast as native Parisians was surely stretching credibility to the breaking point.

Anticipating this problem, Newman attempted to prepare himself for the role of Armand using the same techniques that he had used for *The Outrage*. 'I thought I would attack this one the same way . . . but it doesn't work for this kind of a movie,' Newman confided. 'The more I messed around with tapes of other people and listened to things . . . I just said, " 'Well, I think the thing to do on this one is to have a ball, play it moment to moment, enjoy Sophia Loren and . . . what else must a man do, after all." '

This technique – or lack of it – may have made for an enjoyable couple of months with congenial co-stars, but it didn't make for good reviews. Both the film and its actors were panned unmercifully by critics. *The New Yorker* observed that Newman's performance seemed 'about as far from Paris and anarchism as, say, Akron and the Young Republicans are.' Even the beautiful Sophia Loren, hopelessly miscast, received her share of criticism.

Paul Newman was fortunate in that MGM held back the release of *Lady L* until after the 1966 release of his next film, *Harper*, which was highly successful. Thus Paul was saved the embarrassment of making his fifth disaster in a row since *Hud*.

As he admitted later, Newman realised even as the film was being made that it wasn't working. 'I woke up every morning and knew I wasn't cutting the mustard,' he recalled. Even so, he enjoyed working with Niven, Loren, and especially Ustinov.

'It's marvellous to work with a director who's been an actor, because the lines of communication are closer to being understandable ... it's much easier because he says something to me and I know pretty well what he wants. If I have an objection to something or other, he can absorb that without sort of shaking his head and wiping the flies away,' Paul explained.

Paul Newman reached a milestone during the filming of *Lady L* – he celebrated his 40th birthday on January 26, 1965 in Paris with Peter Ustinov and the other cast members.

Turning 40 is traumatic for many people, especially those whose looks are important to their livelihood or their own self-image and self-esteem. This was not the case with Paul Newman, whose good looks were virtually unchanged from when he was in his twenties. But Paul had an even better reason for feeling young and vital at 40, because in 1965 Joanne gave birth to their third baby, another beautiful little blonde girl, Paul's sixth child and fifth daughter. They named her Claire Olivia, but almost from birth she was known as Clea.

For some years now, Joanne's main function in life was to be a supportive wife to her famous husband and a loving mother to her own children and her stepchildren as well. Her oldest, Nell, was six when Clea was born, and Lissie was four. Now with the new baby, Joanne could count on at least four more years of full-time motherhood.

Although she seldom complained, it would be only natural for a highly creative person like Joanne Woodward to feel resentful at having her own career curtailed during the most vital and productive years of her life. It's a hard job for anyone to be the mother of three young children, and there is really no time or energy left over to be a movie star.

Indeed Joanne herself confirmed this in a 1981 interview in *The New York Times:* 'Initially I probably had a real movie-star dream. It faded somewhere in my mid-thirties when I realised I wasn't going to be that kind of actor. It was painful,' she admitted.

'Also,' she continued, 'I curtailed my career because of the children. Quite a bit. I resented it at the time, which was not a good way to be around the children. Paul was away on location a lot. I wouldn't go on location because of the children. I did once, and felt overwhelmed with guilt.'

But at this time of her life, Joanne was fortunate enough to find a new and exciting interest which was to provide both a physical and creative outlet for years to come. This new pleasure, which soon became almost a passion in Joanne's life, came about when she took her six-year-old daughter Nell for ballet lessons and the teacher suggested that Joanne sign up for an adult ballet class.

Remembering that as a young drama student at the Neighbourhood Playhouse she'd been required to take ballet lessons and that she'd enjoyed them, Joanne decided to give it a try.

'I was 35, really kind of plump around the middle, decidedly middle-aged looking, and I had just had Clea and was nursing her,' Joanne recalled. 'So I started taking ballet, and it was like a drug. I got hooked.'

Lessons twice a week expanded to five times a week, and before long Joanne was taking lessons or practising every day. 'You cannot wait until 35, take up ballet and be a dancer,' she explained. 'I mean, I do a respectable barre ... I have no elevation, but I know what I'm doing, and I can do pique turns around the floor. But I'm the saddest, most frustrated not-quite ballerina there has been for years,' Joanne lamented. 'I wish I had found out at the age of six or seven that I wanted to dance.'

To Joanne at that time, discovering a love for ballet was a godsend. Even if it had come too late for her to develop into a prima ballerina, it gave her an area of interest which she could explore fully, even while being a full-time mother to three – and sometimes six – young children. In time, Joanne's love of ballet would lead her to become actively involved as a leader and fund-raiser for a brave young dance company in Los Angeles.

Chapter 6

The film *Harper* couldn't have come along at a better time in Newman's career. He hadn't had a winner since *Hud*, and if those in the know weren't questioning his versatility as an actor, they were beginning to wonder about his taste in scripts.

Harper was a good antidote to both these implied criticisms of Newman. First, it enabled him to break new ground as an actor and prove himself in a new kind of role – as the hip, cynical, streetwise, brave but vulnerable type of private detective made famous by Humphrey Bogart. The screenplay itself was beyond reproach as well. Adapted by William Goldman from the mystery novel *The Moving Target* by Ross MacDonald, it was suspenseful and excellently written. The characters were interesting and well-defined, and the complicated plot was fast-paced and clearly developed.

Elaine Sampson (Lauren Bacall), a glamorous and wealthy woman aged around 40, contacts Harper, saying that her millionaire husband has been kidnapped and a $500,000 ransom has been demanded. In the course of his investigations, Harper encounters a cross-section of Southern California society, from the upper crust to the underbelly. There is Mrs Sampson's sexy, spoiled step-daughter Miranda (Pamela Tiffin), who is having an affair with Alan Traggert (Robert Wagner), the family pilot. In turn, Traggert is involved with Betty Fraley (Julie Harris), a nightclub singer who is also a junkie. One of the film's more memorable characters is Fay Estabrook (Shelley Winters), a wacky boozing ex-actress who knew Sampson back when, and whose husband is involved in a wetback smuggling operation.

Even while Harper is struggling to unravel the reasons behind the kidnapping and eventual murder, his wife Susan (Janet Leigh) is giving him grief and asks for a divorce. Newman handles the role admirably, showing Harper in all his strengths and weaknesses. He is all too human and at the same time ultimately honourable as he fights his way through the morass of debasing human motives and emotions that have led to this particular crime.

Ross Pelswick in his *New York Journal-America* review said it best: 'Paul Newman checks in just about the best performance of his career ... developed in a mood that's remindful of the early Raymond Chandler, this is a hugely entertaining thriller that manages to come up with suspense and excitement and comedy and yet never gets out of hand ... Newman as the cynical and oh-so-hip Harper is perfectly cast in the role, playing it cool no matter what comes up, tossing off flip lines and slugging it out with the best of them.'

Psychologically this film was good for Newman because it was his first one with Warner Bros. in over seven years. He had returned to his old studio bosses; not only a bigger star but a richer one, due to his own efforts and independent deals he had made. His old enemy, Jack Warner, whom Paul had told off 'early in the game, when I really couldn't afford to tell him off,' visited the *Harper* set, and he and Paul posed together, shaking hands and smiling. But it's said that among friends Newman referred to Jack Warner as a 'vulgarian' and worse, and never forgave him for persistently referring to Joanne as 'Joan'.

This same year, 1966, Newman also starred – along with Julie Andrews – in his first, last and only Alfred Hitchcock movie, *Torn Curtain*. The pairing of director and star turned out not to benefit either one of them. Many reasons were given for the failure of this movie: it was Hitchcock's fiftieth film, and the old guy had 'lost it'; the plot, concerning intrigue behind the Iron Curtain was totally uninteresting, never mind lacking in suspense; Paul Newman had been in a motorcycle accident and therefore didn't have time to rehearse and prepare for the role; Julie Andrews and Paul Newman lacked the savoir faire and romantic chemistry of a couple like Ingrid Bergman and Cary Grant, which was what the film needed.

Torn Curtain was a good learning experience for Newman. When it was over, he made a vow to be more discriminating about his film projects in the future. Up to that point Paul would take on almost any film if he liked the director, the writer, the subject matter − or any of the above. He put the word out that from then on he intended to be more choosy and said that he would have to read and approve the final script before committing himself to any film project.

These resolutions were made by Paul out of personal disdain for *Torn Curtain* − not because it was a financial disaster. Actually, to the surprise of almost everyone, the movie ended up making a lot of money.

For his next film, *Hombre*, Newman and Martin Ritt teamed up again, along with screenwriters Irving Ravetch and Harriet Fran, Jr., who had collaborated on several of Paul's earlier films. This time they adapted an early novel by famed mystery writer Elmore Leonard for the screen. *Hombre* is a story about John Russel (Newman), a white man who had been kidnapped and raised by Apaches. Released into the white man's world, John struggles to adapt to the confusing and alien culture which is his true heritage. In one definitive scene, when a stage coach John is riding on is held up by bandits, he proves himself the most courageous passenger of all.

Although Newman liked the idea of the movie and looked forward to working with his friend Ritt again, the shoot itself proved gruelling. Starting in the Arizona desert and ending at the Bell Ranch in California's craggy Santa Susana Mountains, filming lasted almost five months and went six weeks over schedule. The shooting had been plagued by every disaster imaginable, both natural and manmade: torrential rains, high winds, dust storms, temperatures of over 100 degrees, defective camera equipment which necessitated reshooting scenes, and a bout of 'flu that landed Paul in the hospital for several days.

When reporter Richard Lewis visited Newman on location at the Bell Ranch (a popular site for shooting Westerns that's within commuting distance from Hollywood) he found the actor frustrated and at the end of his tether. His face deeply tanned by the months of blazing sun, the actor cracked open 'cold ones' while he waited for a complicated scene involving horses to be set up. Plagued with not only the endless delays which kept him from his family back in Connecticut, but also by the character of 'Hombre' which he was having trouble getting a grip on, Newman had bitten his nails to the quick.

'I nibble at them when I'm nervous,' he admitted. 'You can generally judge how comfortable I am by the length of my fingernails. Motion pictures today are in as bad shape as the theatre,' he went on, 'in terms of really distinguished pieces of writing. If I waited until I got a good script, I would work about once every three years.'

Paul also took the opportunity to sound off on another of his pet peeves – the way people, women especially, fixate on his looks rather than his talent. 'You work your butt off for 15 years and a lady comes up to you and says: "Take off your glasses so I can see your blue eyes." I have a standard answer for that – "Is that all you think of me?"'

In another way, Newman had ceased to care what most people, even his own peers, thought of him. He had offended many people in Hollywood by his outspoken criticism of the movie capital and its empty values as well as his preference to live far from California. Around this time, his liberal political views and his commitment to the civil rights struggle made him even more of an oddity as a movie star.

By the time *Hombre* was being filmed, Newman had participated in the March on Washington, a fair-housing sit-in in Sacramento, and a rally to promote 'community understanding' in Gadsden, Alabama, led by the Rev. Martin Luther King, Jr.

Newman's films were banned from many Southern theatres during the Gadsden rally, but Paul believed his political views were much more important that film revenues. And, as soon as his film career became successful enough to generate income well above his needs, Newman began to 'put his money where his mouth was' as far as causes he believed in were concerned. To that end, he started the No Sutch Foundations, whose function was to allocate a certain percentage of Paul's income to charities and organisations he wanted to help. In 1965, much of the $100,000 allocated by No Sutch went to the N.A.A.C.P., S.N.C.C., and CORE.

'People in Hollywood come up to me and say, "Why take a chance? Don't make enemies. It can't possibly help you,"' Newman told a *The New York Times* interviewer on the set of *Hombre*. 'My reaction is, "Kiss off." I still have my citizenship papers. Did I lose them when I became an actor? Do I just abdicate? What they're basically asking me to do is be a person without character,' Newman said. 'A person without character has no enemies. So I prefer to have enemies.'

Paul was then – and remains to this day – uncompromising when it comes to his values and beliefs. They, along with his family, are what make life worth living to Paul Newman. As *Hombre* fell more and more behind schedule, Newman grew more and more restive because of the separation from Joanne and the children.

'My wife is sitting up in Connecticut with the six kids saying, "Where the hell is our leader?"' Paul lamented. 'I now should be enjoying the first extended vacation I had planned in 13 years,' he went on. 'To see it chewed away, a quarter day here, a half day there, by illness, bad weather or whatever, really hurts. From now on, two pictures a year and no more,' he vowed, '. . . one in September, one in January.'

Paul did get that well-deserved vacation after *Hombre* finally completed filming. He spent most of it with Joanne and the kids – not only Nell, Lissie and baby Clea, but the children of his first marriage as well. At 16, Scott was already very grown up, and Susie, 13, and Stephanie, 11, were on their way to becoming young ladies. The family spent the warm summer days drifting lazily on their own private stretch of the Aspetuck River in inflatable yellow boats, swimming, or picnicking on the river's grassy banks.

When Paul and Joanne needed time alone together, they'd slip away to the privacy of the barn, which they'd had converted into a screening room as well as guesthouse. And if they wanted a real change of pace, they'd hop into Paul's red Volkswagen (which he enjoyed having contrasted to the Porsches and Mercedes Benzes of his peers) and zip into New York City for an evening of theatre and dinner out, capped off by a romantic night spent in the privacy of their Manhattan *pied à terre*.

The summer flew by all too quickly, and before Paul knew it he was back in Hollywood to begin his next film, *Cool Hand Luke*. A close-up study of a convict in a Florida chain gang, the film came to be known as one of Newman's best. *Cool Hand Luke* was based on a novel by Donn Pearce, who had experienced the horrors of the Southern prison system first-hand. Pearce adapted his novel into a screenplay with the help of Frank R. Pierson and also acted as technical adviser for the film as well as portraying the part of another convict.

In one respect preparing for the role of Luke was easy for Newman, in that Donn Pearce was right there to explain the character in depth and detail and offer advice on how to play him. On the other hand, in order to look convincing as a hardened member of a chain gang, Newman had to undergo some vigorous physical preparation. He worked out with weights and then switched to the actual 'tools of Luke's trade' – a heavy shovel and a pick axe. Newman had to learn the real rhythm of the heavy, monotonous work, as well as get used to walking in chains.

Actually, even though he'd never been a prisoner, Newman could readily identify with the character of Cool Hand Luke, a man who was able to keep his spirit free even while his body was in chains. 'Luke is the ultimate nonconformist and rebel,' Paul said. 'He may be in jail or the Army or whatever, but he's still a free agent.'

Starting as a loner, who is gentle by nature, Luke gradually wins the respect of the other men through his subtle resistance to and subversion of the prison system. Eventually the entire prison is thrown into an uproar.

'Luke is the perfect existential hero,' said Stuart Rosenberg, the young director who won accolades for the taut, tough style he showed in *Cool Hand Luke*, his first film.

Bosley Crowther of *The New York Times* called Paul Newman's acting job in this film 'superb'. Another critic praised him for being able to convincingly play a character who was called upon to be 'funny, stalwart, submissive, defiant, pathetic and eventually tragic.'

In analysing Newman's unique talent for portraying characters like Cool Hand Luke, Jay Cocks said in *Time* magazine: 'These miscreants are not just part of our culture now but almost part of our national character – the hero as romantic screw-up, the loner crabbed by society and usually, despite his looks, not very lucky with women. The purest and most consistent of these Newman voices is the sweet-natured convict hero of Stuart Rosenberg's *Cool Hand Luke*, released in 1967. Luke is not very bright, but he is an original,' Cocks goes on, 'and the scene in which he brags that he can eat 50 eggs, and then proves it, is marvellous comedy. There is a powerful sadness when fumblingly he plays "Plastic Jesus" on the banjo after his mother's death, and when he is ground to his inevitable death by the vicious prison system, the waste of a gentle man.'

Never one to rest on his laurels – and he received praise of the highest order for *Cool Hand Luke* – Newman was soon busy making a new movie. Even though it was directed by Jack Smight who had done such a good job with *Harper*, this film was another silly and unlikely farce of the type that had always proved disastrous to Newman.

If the film's title weren't enough to warn off most people – *The Secret War of Harry Frigg* – a plot synopsis would be. Harry Frigg is a bumbling private in World War II Europe. After managing to escape from the stockades, he is sent on a top-secret mission to rescue four Allied generals from the Axis prison where they are being held. This turns out to be a fortified castle where, after gaining entrance, Harry Frigg falls in love with the resident countess (Sylvia Koscina), to the detriment of his rescue operation.

Needless to say, the critics had a field day with this one. Not only was the title taken to task for being a cheap box office ploy, and not only was the plot criticised for being far-fetched and silly – but once again Newman's inability to play farce was commented upon.

After *Harry Frigg*, a change of pace was definitely needed by Newman, but even he couldn't have anticipated the amazing change which his next film project brought about. First of all, Paul didn't even act in the film – he directed it. And the female star who dominated the picture from first frame to last was none other than his own wife, Joanne Woodward. Naturally the film was *Rachel, Rachel*, made by the Newman's in the summer of 1967.

For years Newman had harboured a desire to try his hand at directing. He had studied the techniques of directing years before while enrolled at Yale Drama School. And actually he *had* directed a short film (28 minutes) in 1961 – *On the Harmfulness of Tobacco* – adapted from the Chekhov story of the same name. It had one cast member, Michael Strong, and its run at the Sutton Theatre in New York lasted two days.

Even so, Newman called it 'the best creation experience I've ever had. I was just absolutely alive,' he explained. 'My wife must have thought I was on drugs.'

In explaining his urge to direct, he said, 'If you were a painter and you were allowed only one quarter of a canvas, it would be a disappointment. Why merely be a first violinist if you can conduct?'

Very likely Paul's ambition to direct would have remained just a fantasy for many more years if it hadn't been for Joanne's old friend and agent, John Forman, reading a certain book, liking it, and recommending it to Joanne. The book, *A Jest of God* by a Canadian writer, Margaret Laurence, had won the Governor General's award, which is similar to the American Pulitzer Prize. Paul wasn't overly impressed after reading the book himself, but Joanne liked it enough to take an option on the book, which eventually became the film *Rachel, Rachel*.

As Paul once said of his wife, 'Joanne is the only one I trust about what parts to take. Her taste is impeccable.' And as *Rachel, Rachel* was to prove, her taste in books and screenplays was excellent, too.

'People kept asking, "Whatever happened to Joanne Woodward?" Well, she got bored waiting around. That's why I was attracted to *Rachel, Rachel*,' the actress said. 'It's theme is that things never stop, tomorrow is another day. I felt very unhappy and discouraged and I felt my career had ended. I'm not a movie star anyway. I've never been the same person twice on screen and Hollywood never really knew what to do with me, so when you're in that boat, you either become an enormously successful established character actress or you do anything you can get.

'I was determined I'd rather do nothing than just work for the sake of having a job, and I was even more determined I'd never do anything again unless I felt strongly about it. One day John Forman called ...'

Joanne asked a close friend of theirs, writer Stewart Stern, to do a screenplay based on *A Jest of God*. He had done the screenplays for *The Rack*, an early film of Newman's and for the famous *Rebel Without a Cause*. He was as enthusiastic as Joanne was about *A Jest of God* as a film property and wrote the screenplay on speculation.

Then the really hard part came – trying to find a film company that was interested. 'Paul had no intention of directing it, but we couldn't get anyone else interested,' Joanne explained. 'Stewart Stern, who wrote the screenplay, and I went around offering ourselves to everybody, but I'm afraid offering a package of the script and me was hardly like offering Elizabeth Taylor and Tennessee Williams.'

With Paul Newman finally committed to directing the project, they eventually found a backer – Warners-Seven Arts. 'We had a $700,000 budget, and anything over the budget came out of my pocket, my after-tax pocket, so it was twice as painful,' Paul said. 'My wife and I took no salaries at all, but if the picture ever goes into a profit position she and I and Stewart will split three ways. I must say, by way of applause to Seven Arts, which put up the money, that I had nobody breathing down my neck,' Paul added. 'They were willing to take a gamble.'

To produce a film like *Rachel, Rachel* in a Hollywood studio would have cost over $2 million and their budget was a third of that. To keep costs down, the Newmans decided to make the film in Connecticut and set the story there as well. They found an old gymnasium in Danbury and converted it into a workable studio and sound stage. Good outside shots were readily available in the picturesque town, and Paul used local people not only as extras, but also to play small parts in the film. Costs were further kept down by condensing the shooting schedule into five weeks.

Paul made a point of contacting people in various areas of film who he had worked with in the past. He wanted not only people with expertise, but also people he felt might be interested in the film artistically. The enthusiasm he and Joanne felt communicated itself to others involved. To almost everyone who helped make it, *Rachel, Rachel* became a labour of love.

Paul succeeded in hiring Dede Allen, one of the industry's best film editors, who was there from the onset, as was Stewart Stern, in case any last minute script changes had to be made. Estelle Parsons, probably the best known cast member outside Joanne, was glad to contribute her talents to the film. 'I don't communicate too well with directors, but he's wonderful,' she said of Paul. 'It has all been so relaxed and easy.'

'It was sort of a family affair,' Paul said of *Rachel, Rachel*. 'My daugher Nell is in it – as a parent I was against that, but as a director I thought she was great – and so is Frank Corsaro, who directed us in *Baby Want a Kiss*, and so is my auto mechanic. I had a marvellous crew,' Paul went on. 'The first day of shooting I said to them, "I'm a virgin and I need your help," and they were so first-class I couldn't believe it.'

Newman and many people who know him look back with almost a sense of wonder that he dared to attempt a project like this in the first place. Close friend Stewart Stern had the best explanation to offer when he said of Paul: 'He's the only man I ever met who decides what makes him nervous – like directing a movie – and then, with his hands sweating and his feet sweating, goes right into it.'

And then Stern makes it touchingly clear that in this project as in so many other, Joanne Woodward was Paul's inspiration. 'Paul has a real sense of adoration for what Joanne can do,' Stern said. 'He's constantly trying to provide a setting where the world can see what he sees in her.'

Rachel, Rachel did turn out to be the perfect showcase for Joanne's delicate but deeply felt and emotionally compelling acting talents. The plot of the film is spare and static, having to do mainly with the inner life of a sexually repressed small town schoolteacher and what happens to her after she surrenders her virginity in what turns out to be a one-night stand. Would anyone, especially in the politically turbulent late 1960s go to see a film that was as simple and as limited in scope as this? Paul Newman and Joanne Woodward didn't know – but they were damned well going to try to make *Rachel, Rachel* a film they could be proud of.

At 35, Rachel Cameron (Woodward) hasn't yet had sex with a man. Her life, severely limited in scope and possibility, is made up of the small town she lives in, the young children she teaches, and her petulant, demanding mother (Kate Harrington) with whom she lives. Her friends are few – the neighbourhood undertaker (Frank Corsaro) and another female schoolteacher, Calla (played by Estelle Parsons).

Rachel realises that her time of life is crucial. 'I'm in the exact middle of my life,' she tells Calla. 'This is my last ascending summer.'

In an attempt to break through the repression that has kept her life frozen, Rachel agrees to go to a revival meeting with Calla. The female preacher (Geraldine Fitzgerald) urges the congregation into a shouting, singing frenzy, and Calla explains this always gives her an emotional lift. The hysterical interlude makes Rachel feel good too – until after the prayer meeting when Calla makes a lesbian pass at her.

Rachel knows this is not the answer to her problems, but her wish for something to happen to her – finally – makes her easy prey for Nick (James Olson), a childhood pal who is a teacher in the city but has come back to his parents' farm for the summer. Rachel accepts a date with him and during a walk in the woods loses her virginity to him. They spend the weekend together, Rachel enjoys the first real sexual and emotional abandon of her life – and then Nick leaves her. Through certain physical symptoms, Rachel believes that she is pregnant. Upset at first, she then welcomes the idea of having a child of her own, only to find out that what is growing inside of her is a benign cyst, not a baby. She has it removed during an operation, and then, ultimately glad rather than sorry for what has happened, she announces to her mother that they are moving to Oregon. In some deep way, the sexual fling has freed Rachel from her repression, and she is ready to try life in a different place, and on her own terms.

This film, which is essentially the portrait of a woman's life during one summer, is augmented by both flashbacks and flashforwards which represent Rachel's memories of her fantasies. Some of her more memorable flashbacks are of her father, an undertaker, who died 14 years before and whom Rachel adored. The young Rachel (played by Nell Newman who looks like Joanne except for a pair of piercingly blue eyes inherited from her father), sneaks into her father's mortuary, both frightened and fascinated by the lifeless bodies. Perhaps in her mind death came to represent peacefulness; at any rate, the mature Rachel often fantasises scenarios of her own death.

Paradoxically, *Rachel, Rachel,* which concerns sexual repression, is actually more open about sexual matters than most films made around that time. For instance, Rachel is shown masturbating under the covers at bedtime. But even as she writhes with release, she murmurs guiltily to herself, 'It's just to make me sleep . . .' Even now, how many films dare approach the still-sensitive subject of adult masturbation?

Looking at the sexual subject matter of *Rachel, Rachel* from a lighter point of view, many people wondered how it felt for Paul Newman to direct his wife in love scenes with another man. 'Friends always ask about the love scenes,' Paul said, 'and I've got a pat answer: "If she's in bed with another actor, I put her there!"'

In terms of Paul directing his wife in a film, and Joanne being directed by her husband, they both found the experience to be an unqualified success.

'My wife is in it,' Paul said in *The New York Times,* before *Rachel, Rachel* came out. 'She's brilliant . . . marvellous. We have the same acting vocabularies and that made it a hell of a lot easier,' he went on. 'I just gave her one-line zingers, like "pinch it" or "thicken it" and she knew what I meant. I can't think of any other actress that the experience of directing could have been better with,' Paul finished glowingly.

Joanne's praise for her husband was just as unqualified: 'With all due respect to the other wonderful directors I've ever worked with,' she said, 'it was just heaven to work with Paul.'

To Paul and Joanne, *Rachel, Rachel* was a 'success' from the start, because it was a project they both believed in. After working so well together as director and actress, they were even more encouraged. The production moved along swiftly and serenely, and with very few hitches to hold it up, it was completed on schedule. But then the 'moment of truth' came, at least as far as the critics were concerned. Would *Rachel, Rachel* be appreciated for what it was the way Paul and Joanne had appreciated it from the start? In other words, had they succeeded in translating what they had felt and believed about it to the screen? Even if the critics did like it, would the public go to see it?

The answers to those questions were very important to the Newmans, but not for any reason that had to do with money.

'I hope it's successful,' said Paul, 'not because of any financial rewards – hell, both Joanne and I did it for nothing – but to prove to Hollywood you can make a film about basic, simple people, without violence and a band of Indians scalping the settlers.'

'It just had to work,' Joanne said fervently. 'If *Rachel* had been totally unsuccessful, I would have been heartbroken – not for me but because we had filmed every bit of our insides, and it would have hurt if people hadn't like it.'

Rachel, Rachel turned out to be an unqualified success, not only with the critics but the public, too. The best thing was that Paul and Joanne could share the praise equally (there was plenty to go around) just the way they had shared equally in bringing *Rachel, Rachel* to the screen.

Discriminating movie and theatre-goers had always known

that Joanne Woodward was a gifted actress – at least since *Three Faces of Eve* was released and won her the best actress award. But those who had perhaps forgotten how talented she was were reminded upon the release of *Rachel, Rachel*.

'Joanne Woodward has never been better,' Archer Winston wrote in the *New York Post*. 'In fact, she may never have been quite this good, so deeply, simply touching.'

Richard Schickel in his review in *Life* magazine said, 'Miss Woodward demonstrates again that she is perhaps the only major female star of our day capable of genuine naturalism, submerging self and image in a subtle, disciplined performance that avoids showiness, excessive sentiment, self-consciousness.'

In terms of Paul Newman, Schickel said, 'As a director, Newman is anything but the bouncing boy-o we are accustomed to seeing on our screens. He has a sensitive, slightly melancholic eye for something most American movies miss – the texture of ordinary life. He displays, moreover, a feel for emotional nuance and a technical sureness; he is neither too radical nor too conservative. This is remarkable in a first film,' Schickel concludes.

As if these reviews weren't glowing enough, the ultimate accolade of the blending of both Paul and Joanne's talents in *Rachel, Rachel* was given by noted reviewer, Judith Crist: '. . . it was easy to forget in the eleven years since *Eve* not merely the dramatic range of which Miss Woodward is capable but also the astonishing ability she has of transfiguring herself in the course of it. This ability is beautifully exploited in her portrait of the 35-year-old spinster . . . taking a chance on the living that she has shielded herself from and facing the consequences. The exploitation is in no small part to Mr Newman's credit,' she goes on. 'There is no facet of the lonely, repressed and introverted woman that is not probed by both actress and director and probed with a deep understanding. What might have been trite and maudlin becomes in their hands an illumination of universal experience; the essence of sensitive living, of an awareness of the loser's battle so many of us wage in our very existence . . .'

Needless to say, Joanne in particular was thrilled by the enthusiastic reception of what had been her 'brain child'. 'I guess *Rachel* has revived my career,' the actress said. 'Some people thought I'd gone underground.'

It gave her the hope of being able to work more often in the future. 'I only do a picture about every two or three years. I seem to have babies in between,' she said, glancing teasingly at her husband. 'Now I'd like to be more active, principally because I feel I've done my bit for the population explosion and raised my children to where I feel I'm not depriving them if I'm working.'

'Joanne really gave up her career for me, to stick by me, to make the marriage work,' Paul added. 'That's one of the reasons I directed this film with her.'

And now that *Rachel, Rachel* had proved itself both an artistic and a commercial success, no one could have been prouder of Joanne Woodward than her husband Paul.

Chapter 7

People had been curious about the Newman marriage eve. since they tied the knot on January 29, 1958, thereby 'legitimising' their long-standing romance. Were the couple really as in love as they seemed? Even if they were, could the marriage survive the pressures of show business and the separations and temptations presented by not only one but two movie careers? Besides all that, Newman was one of the handsomest male actors around. All he'd have to do would be to wink one of those devastating blue eyes and hundreds of women would come running. Joanne was pretty enough, but she'd had three kids in seven years, the gossips noted, and everyone knew what *that* could do to your figure, never mind your frame of mind. Could a woman really feel sexy and desirable and in the mood for fun and romance with all those kids underfoot?

But, while gossips predicted the worst, and friends and fans hoped for the best, the Newmans remained oblivious to it all. Scrupulously guarding their privacy, granting interviews only when they were excited about a new film project, the Newmans went about their business – and their marriage survived.

It was 1968 and they had been married ten years when Paul made the first definitive statements about his and Joanne's private life and marriage.

When asked if there was any friction between himself and

his wife during the filming of *Rachel, Rachel,* Newman replied, 'Oh, yeah. We had several spats and squabbles – big ones. There are never little ones in our family. But it had nothing to do with work,' he added. 'In terms of actually working, Joanne and I never had one harsh word in that entire period. It was really amazing . . . The marvellous thing about our working together is basically that we trust each other.'

When asked whether their marriage was as successful as it was reputed to be, Paul said, 'Well, as I just pointed out, it's not always fine and dandy – it involves two people with very different approaches and attitudes to things – but I think it has a certain thickness to it. We go through periods where we think we're bad parents and periods where we think we see each other only as reflections of ourselves – all the usual jazz. But there's affection and respect and a good deal of humour.'

He also attributed the success of their marriage to the fact that they hadn't been separated too frequently – and he gave Joanne most of the credit for this. 'She's had many opportunities to go abroad or on location by herself,' Paul said, 'and she's turned these offers down in order to stay with me. She's done this to the detriment of her career, I'm afraid, but it's helped to keep us together.'

Still another ingredient to their matrimonial longevity, Paul believed, was their avoidance of the social whirl enjoyed by most celebrities. For instance, he said that a party they gave for Gore Vidal on his return from Europe was the first and only party he and Joanne had thrown for ten years!

'That's how social we are,' Paul said wryly. 'Even if we *were* social, we wouldn't have time for it,' he pointed out. 'When you're raising three children continuously and six part of the time, and you've got a couple of houses to run . . . and you still want to have a career, it's kind of tough to remain in good standing with the beautiful people. In other words, it's not a glamorous Hollywood marriage.'

Paul wasn't complaining when he made that final statement. In fact, he was implying that if he and Joanne had not given their family life first priority their marriage may not have lasted as long as it had. One can't help wondering if Paul would have been surprised to learn in 1968 that twenty years later in 1988 his marriage would still be going strong!

The title of their subsequent film, in which the Newmans starred together, couldn't have been more appropriate. *Winning*, a story about sports car racers, appealed to both of them. Paul himself had always been interested in the sport, and Joanne liked both the script and the human drama present in the plot. Since this involved her in a triangle situation with both her husband and Robert Wagner, who could blame her?

The story is about a top racer, Frank Capua (Newman) who marries a woman, Elora (Joanne Woodward), the mother of a teenaged son (Richard Thomas). However, their family life is gradually eroded by Frank's obsession with racing, which keeps him almost constantly away from home. Feeling neglected, Elora turns to another driver (Robert Wagner) who is Frank's main opponent in a big upcoming race. Adding to Frank's humiliation is the fact that his wife's lover has been offered the car he himself had hoped to drive in the race.

The teenage son stands by his stepfather, helping him to rebuild his own car and ready it for the big race. Against tremendous odds, Frank comes in first, but the victory seems curiously empty and he realises that human relationships are what really matter. To that end, with his stepson's encouragement, he goes after a reconciliation with Elora.

Universal Studios spared no expenses in this production of *Winning*, spending $7 million, but this was one example of money spent to good effect. For instance, footage of a 17-car crash which occurred during a real Indianapolis 500 race was incorporated into the film, and care was taken to make the car racing scenes authentic in every way. As a matter of fact, during the filming, Paul fell in love with the sport to such an extent that he insisted on doing all of his character's driving chores himself, without the use of a double. Concerned about the safety of their leading man, Universal allowed it – after insuring Newman for $1 million.

Within a week of its release, *Winning* had proved itself a winner. A good script and good actors involved in an action-filled plot, along with a love story that contained its own element of suspense, made *Winning* triumph at the box office. It easily made up the hefty sum spent on its production and went on to earn profits over and above its initial investment.

Winning also garnered good reviews for the Newmans. Howard Thompson in *The New York Times* called it: 'Probably the best-rounded and most appealing personalised film of this kind ever made ... The Newmans are both splendid.'

Variety gave Paul nothing short of a rave review, saying: 'Newman underplays his part throughout, resulting in one of his better performances. He is ideally cast as the racer, and those sequences in which he is racing are convincingly portrayed.'

For Paul Newman, *Winning* turned out to be much more than a film he enjoyed making and one which earned him good reviews. In fact, *Winning* changed his life in a very significant way: it instilled in Paul a love for sports cars and racing which endures to this very day. Most sports car racers reach their peak about age 44, but that is the age at which Newman took up this fast and dangerous sport. In fact, his love of the sport amounted to almost an addiction to speed.

'I first learned to drive fast for *Winning*,' he told *The New York Times* interviewer. 'Up to then I'd done nothing more dangerous than driving the highway from Connecticut where I live, into New York in a souped-up Volkswagen with a Porsche engine.

'I didn't plunge into the high speeds all at once,' he explained. 'It's like those guys who fall free; they start in at just a few thousand feet and work up. I began by driving at 80, then I'd go up to 90 and 120. Finally ... I went up to 185. The cars I was driving were only supposed to go at 120 miles

Paul and Joanne's marriage in Las Vegas in 1958.

Paul with Leon Uris in Israel in 1960 while filming *Exodus*.

Paul directed Joanne in *Rachel, Rachel* in 1968.

Paul with his son Scott, who died of a drugs overdose in 1978.

Paul and Joanne attend an Academy Awards ceremony in 1984 with Susan Kendall, F daughter from his first marriage.

an hour, and that was a helluva risk. The insurance guys were crapping in their pants!'

It would still be a while before sports car racing would become almost a second career with Newman, dominating each year from April to October. By the time he reached his late forties, Paul would become one of the top drivers on the amateur circuit.

Meantime, as later assessments would show, Newman was still on his way to becoming one of the top actors in the movie business. Of course, Paul's talent had been there all along, more visible and compelling in some of his films (24 up to then) than in others. But many believe that starting with his next movie, *Butch Cassidy and the Sundance Kid*, Newman hit his full stride as an actor.

Butch Cassidy and the Sundance Kid is a uniquely American film – a lighthearted Western about two lovable outlaws in the early days of this century. The era of the 'wild West' is ending, this breed of outlaw is becoming extinct, and this adds to the poignancy of the film. There is a real sense of nostalgia present, with Butch and the Kid seeming to be caught photographically in a fleeting moment of time. Just the mention of this movie is enough to bring a smile to the face of anyone who has seen it. That, along with its hit song, 'Raindrops Keep Falling on my Head' by Burt Bacharach makes it a likely candidate for most people's list of favourite films.

The film, released by 20th Century-Fox, was essentially the brainchild of the brilliantly creative George Roy Hill, who along with Paul Monach had formed a production company. The captivating screenplay, which is so crucial to the film's lighthearted comedic tone, was written by William Goldman, who also did the screenplay for *Harper*. Goldman based the screenplay of *Butch Cassidy and the Sundance Kid* on authentic files from the Pinkerton Detective Agency, which had hunted the two outlaws for years, but he softened the characters considerably. In real life, Butch Cassidy was a desperate outlaw and the Kid was a trigger-happy killer.

In the film, the two are portrayed as essentially innocent, perennial adolescents who rob trains good-naturedly and don't mean any real harm to anyone. In fact, when the head of the Union Pacific railroad sends heavy-duty federal agents after them, Butch and the Kid are actually indignant.

The plot of *Butch Cassidy* is much less important to the film than the rakish charm and reckless bravado of a outlaws themselves. In it, Butch Cassidy (Newman), leader of the Wyoming gang known as the Hole in the Wall Gang or the Wild Bunch meets up with one of the wild West's most notorious young outlaws, the Sundance Kid. They start robbing trains for a living, getting into a number of comical scrapes along the way. The Kid is romantically involved with a young Denver school-teacher, Etta Place (Katherine Ross), and when the Feds are sent after them, they go on the run across country, taking Etta with them.

Hearing (wrongly) that Bolivia offers opportunities for a pair of enterprising young outlaws like themselves, Butch, Etta and the Kid head to South America. Once in Bolivia, they find that times are hard and both the natives and the terrain are inimical to their interests. Against Etta's wishes, they persist in their dangerous outlaw doings, and finally she sadly bids farewell to them rather than risk seeing them brought down.

But brought down they are. Caught in a cul-de-sac trap in a mean Bolivian town, they come out of their hiding place, guns blazing at the soldiers who greatly outnumber them. The film ends – brilliantly – in a freeze frame, so that we don't have to watch the sad slaughter of our brave and endearing heroes.

In *Butch Cassidy*, Newman continued with his new technique, first commented upon in *Winning*, in which he was said to 'underplay' his role.

In fact, according to Lawrence J. Quirk in *Screen Slants*, 'Newman is so effacing that he virtually hands the film to

Redford ... Newman performs in a delightfully light and at times even fey style, underplaying shrewdly, essaying comedy scenes (like a trick bicycle-riding sequence) with an ease and an insouciance I have never seen him display in such measure ...Newman's style here is (I suspect deliberately) more subtly muted and nimbly self-effacing.'

Many years later when Newman was asked for his own personal assessment of *Butch Cassidy and the Sundance Kid*, he was to call it, 'A delight. Too bad they got killed at the end, 'cause those two guys could have gone on in films forever,' he added, echoing the sentiments of everyone who loved the charming and nostalgic film.

Newman's next film, *WUSA*, was undertaken as a kind of political crusade by Paul: Joanne, who also starred in it; Stuart Rosenberg, who directed it; and John Forman, the Newmans' old friend who was involved with them as co-producer on some films. Based on a novel, *Hall of Mirrors*, by Robert Stone, who also wrote the screenplay, *WUSA* tells the story of an itinerant disc jockey who gets caught up in the political activities of a Southern radio station and in right-wing politics which in his case reach neo-fascist proportions.

The cast of *WUSA* was strong, including in addition to the Newmans – Anthony Newley, Laurence Harvey, Pat Hingle and Cloris Leachman, but even so the critics attacked the film with a vengeance. Paramount, which had hoped the controversial nature of the film would attract the public instead of repelling it, swiftly curtailed its distribution.

Newman, who genuinely believed that the film accurately reflected red-neck politics and neo-fascist tendencies in America, was at first furious at the way *WUSA* was rejected by the critics.

'I hope the European reviews are good,' he said. 'Perhaps they'll see it's a portrait of the way America is run. I'd like to see an ad in all the newspapers and magazines here with the European raves and say to the lousy critics in the East, "Look at this!"'

But in time Newman began to realise that perhaps the film had not succeeded in accurately reflecting the political situation in America – at least not in a way that made sense to the public at large. Several years later, he was to look back at *WUSA* and call it, 'A film of incredible potential . . . We tried to make it political, and it wasn't.'

Paul Newman's next screen project started out as another Newman-Forman project, with Richard Colla directing. *Sometimes a Great Notion* was based on the novel of the same name by the off-beat but talented author Ken Kesey, who also wrote *One Flew Over the Cuckoo's Nest*. John Gay wrote the screenplay for *Sometimes a Great Notion*, which concerns the adventures and misadventures of the Stampers, an eccentric family of lumberjacks in Oregon. Dominated by their patriarch (Henry Fonda), the enclave includes the elder son Jack (Paul Newman) and a nephew Joe Bert (Richard Jaeckel), along with their wives, who all live under Pa Stamper's thumb both at home and at work. When a general strike hits the logging camp where the Stamper men work, they exercise their family motto, 'Don't give an inch' and continue to chop down trees.

Meantime there is trouble on the home front too in the shape of Leeland, younger son of Pa Stamper and half-brother Jack. He has a mass of grievances against his father concerning his mother, and it doesn't help matters when he takes up with Jack's discontented wife (Lee Remick). Tragedy inevitably ensues, but it doesn't break the spirit or the family continuity of this strong-minded backwoods clan.

From the start Newman was excited about doing the film and portraying the pivotal role of Jack, the elder son. As it turned out, he ended up directing the film as well, due both to clashes with the original director and a broken ankle on Newman's part which necessitated closing down the project at a crucial time.

'I wanted to do the picture because, like so many of my best pictures – I'm thinking of *Hud* and *Hombre* especially – it shows the life of simple Americans,' Paul told an interviewer. 'There are wonderful things in it. Hank Fonda has a death scene that is one of the finest things I ever saw. I fired the director after three weeks,' Paul continued, 'because he didn't understand the subject in the way I thought he should and I took over the directing, because how could you find a new guy in Hollywood and train him to understand the logging business in three weeks?' Paul asked, shrugging.

Still obviously smarting from the unpopularity of his last film, though protesting the opposite, Newman said, 'After *WUSA* I wouldn't exactly be asked to the White House. It was a good deal too frank about right-wing demagoguery, but *Notion* will probably be seen with murmurs of approval from the onlookers in the Oval Office, it's so much a picture of grassroots America. Not that I give a damn either way. I don't care for Washington's opinion,' he claimed, 'and I don't care for New York's.'

As it happened, *Sometimes a Great Notion* was appreciated by the New York critics – not only for the performances of Henry Fonda and Newman in particular, but for Newman's direction as well.

'Newman is better than he has been in years as the favourite son who idolises his father . . . Fonda, as the old man . . . has a death scene that must stand among the best work of a lifetime filled with superb film acting,' Jay Cocks wrote in *Time*.

And Judith Crist, that grande dame of reviewers, said in *New York* magazine that '. . . one must credit Newman as director, for in this second demonstration of his skill, he shows that he can go beyond that introspection and sensitivities of *Rachel, Rachel,* and deal with the harsh primitivism of man and nature.'

The next person in the Newman family to do a movie was Joanne, who starred in *They Might Be Giants.* She played a psychiatrist with George C. Scott as an intriguing and mystifying patient who almost takes over her life. While this film didn't enjoy popular success, it was well-liked by students and intellectuals who appreciated *avant garde* cinema. In fact *They Might Be Giants* can be considered one of the few American films that could qualify in this category.

1971 brought forth a new trend on the part of the Newmans: they decided to appear occasionally on television. They had both found work on early live television when they'd each arrived in New York, so it was a return to a familiar medium.

Now as established stars, they chose to do television projects when something especially interesting was offered. In April, Paul appeared as the host and star of *Once Upon a Wheel*, an ABC-TV special on sports car racing which cost $400,000 to produce. Paul, who had been fascinated by the sport since starring in *Winning*, had become an expert on it.

Once Upon a Wheel was a perfect project for Newman, since it entailed getting paid for two of the things he loved best: talking about car racing, and driving souped-up vehicles at mind-blowing speeds. The TV special gave Paul a chance to learn even more about his favourite sport during segments filmed on location at various speedtracks such as the Ontario Motor Speedway in California, the Indianapolis Speedway, the Soap Box Derby in Ohio, as well as tracks in Europe. He also got to try his hand at racing, along with other daring stars such as James Garner, Kirk Douglas and Glenn Ford.

Joanne Woodward's appearance on TV in November of the same year couldn't have been more different. Just as Paul's foray into car racing enabled him to indulge in his love for speed, Joanne's special, *All the Way Home*, allowed her to indulge in her love for fine drama. This dramatic version of the James Agee novel, *A Death in the Family* was adapted by the Pulitzer Prize-winning playwright Tad Mosel. It starred Pat Hingle, Eileen Heckart, and Richard Kiley as well as Joanne as the bereaved wife and widowed mother. To add to Joanne's enjoyment, the play was directed by her old friend from early TV, Fred Coe, and was produced by David Susskind.

At about the time she taped this TV play, Joanne was 41 but looked to be in her mid-twenties. When asked by an interviewer what she attributed her youthful appearance to, Joanne replied, 'It's hard to say. I look at my face in the mirror all the time, searching for signs. I'd hate to have one of those faces, like some actors and actresses do, that suddenly disintegrates. Paul who is 46, and I are like Bobbsey Twins,' she went on. 'We think everybody gets old but us.'

Joanne also mentioned at this time that she and Paul had decided to put their Beverly Hills house up for sale. 'Between the smog and the last earthquake, I finally made up my mind,' she said. 'I thought how perfectly absurd it is to have a beautiful home and have to drive weekends to the beach so my child, who is allergic to the smog, can breathe, and on top of it almost be victimised by an earthquake,' Joanne finished, shaking her head.

Paul agreed with his wife. Coming off *Sometimes a Great Notion* and being in a wild mood, he said: 'I hate Los Angeles because of the deadly smog. I want to go to Australia and live by my wits with just a little food and water, and see if I can really be a pioneer. Wouldn't that be a good life for a son of a bitch?'

In 1972, another production company which Newman had formed with Sidney Poitier and Barbra Streisand some years before and which they named First Artists, finally produced its first film. One of Newman's least known films, it was called *Pocket Money* and featured himself and Lee Marvin as a pair of bumbling, not-too-bright con artists. The two stars worked well together as a team and no one could really explain why the film didn't work.

'I loved the character; the script didn't come together, though,' Paul Newman remarked later.

Stuart Rosenberg, who had directed Paul in the excellent *Cool Hand Luke*, couldn't save this film, which the critics dismissed as a failed attempt to create a *Butch Cassidy and the Sundance Kid* type film.

Later in 1972, First Artists launched another Paul Newman film. Clumsily titled *The Life and Times of Judge Roy Bean*, it was another Western (that genre had always been pretty lucky for Paul), set in the late 1800s. Perhaps the film's greatest drawing card for Paul was that it was to be directed by John Huston. Together, First Artists and Huston assembled a great cast, including Jacqueline Bisset, Tab Hunter, Stacy Keach, Anthony Perkins and Victoria Principal.

The film was shot on location in the Arizona desert and it took ten weeks to complete. Newman was not only in every scene – but for much of the time, his co-star was a large mountain bear whose moods were 'unpredictable'. It surely must have been owing to Huston and the rest of the cast that Paul called making the film 'the most delightful experience of my professional life.'

The storyline of *The Life and Times of Judge Roy Bean* is bizarre and far-fetched, to say the least. It's described as 'an American Western fantasy' and takes place in a small, imaginary Texas town named Langtry, after the famous Lily Langtry. Roy Bean arrives in Langtry and through a case of mistaken identity he is beaten and then condemned to a public hanging. But on the scaffold, a miracle takes place – the rope snaps just at the right moment and Bean survives. He plots his revenge, finally coming back to kill everyone who was responsible for his ordeal.

'The first three quarters of the picture is classic,' Newman said later. 'We never came to grips with the ending, though. I loved that character,' he added incongruously.

Surely, the film and especially its ending were a strange choice on Newman's part. He had always claimed to abhor violence, but the part of Bean would have been more suitable for John Wayne. Perhaps Newman was so intrigued at the idea of working with Huston that he decided to overlook the film's violent and meaningless ending.

At any rate, Huston and Newman were among the very few

people who liked the film. The critics jumped all over it, justifiably in this case, and it failed badly at the box office, being Newman's fourth failure in a row since *Butch Cassidy*.

Perhaps Paul felt that he needed a break from acting at this point. Or maybe the luck and good timing he was famous for had operated once again. At any rate, just at that time Joanne and Paul happened upon a film property that would be perfect for them to collaborate on. She would star in it, and he would direct.

Chapter 8

The Effect of Gamma Rays on Man-in-the-Moon Marigolds was the ungainly but certainly intriguing title of the next film Paul and Joanne did together. The title was retained from the Pulitzer Prize-winning play by Paul Zindel, which was produced off-Broadway with Sada Thompson in the leading role.

The set-up of filming *Marigolds* was similar to that of *Rachel, Rachel* in several ways. The cast was small, with Joanne dominating as Beatrice Hunsdorfer, a neurotic, unfulfilled shrew whose mood swings keep her two young daughters on an emotional roller coaster. One of these daughters (who is second only to the character of Beatrice in importance) was also an alumna of *Rachel, Rachel* – the Newmans' own daughter, Nell, now 13. In the credits of both films, she is listed as Nell Potts, which evolved from a childhood nickname, 'Nell-potts.' Rounding out the small cast was Roberta Wallach, the daughter of another talented acting team, Eli Wallach and Anne Jackson.

Also, *Marigolds* was filmed near the Newmans' home base, in Bridgeport, Connecticut. They used the parsonage of an abandoned church, which was soon to be torn down for the sake of urban renewal. What wasn't already dingy enough in the house was made dingier by the crew. In the 'parlour', the walls are a drab brown, the furniture is dilapidated – and every surface is littered with papers, leftover meals and general junk. The only bright spot is a tray of orange marigolds massed in front of one window. These, the main symbol of the film, are being grown by the young daughter (Nell) for a junior high school science project.

'The house had Joanne in a depressed state,' said Paul, after putting in an especially rough day as director.

Actually, it was the role itself that depressed Joanne, including both the way she looked as Beatrice, and the way her character acted. 'In *Marigolds*,' she told Rex Reed, 'I was supposed to be one of the frowziest hags in town. All the clothes were my mother's, because she's a pack rat and never throws anything away, so I went through her closet and dragged out a lot of old junk and dyed it in icky colours and wore it,' Joanne explained. 'I was so depressed . . . during that film, I couldn't stand it.'

And who could blame Joanne for feeling that way when on a typical day of filming, her wardrobe consisted of a shabby maroon bathrobe, a pair of white nylon socks and green corduroy slippers? She was allowed no make-up, and as for her mousy hair, Joanne says, 'I hated that gooky rinse they put on my hair that got all over the pillowcase at night. I hated the way I looked, and I hated the character and what she did to those children. I don't look or act like that,' Joanne went on, 'but let's face it − nobody is going to . . . cast me as a 43-year-old sex symbol.'

While on the set of *Marigolds*, Paul said almost the same thing: 'In order to survive in motion pictures, I have to wear a couple of hats. The roles available to me as an actor now are fewer and fewer. But I was a directing major at Yale, you know . . . With *Rachel*, I got pushed into directing.'

Reading between the lines, one realises that, starting almost at this exact point in their careers, they had to stop picking and choosing when it came to plum roles, and at times settle for whatever was offered to them, even if the film project wasn't geared to their own personal and artistic tastes.

In terms of *Marigolds*, Paul said, 'I did have certain script restrictions as a director. I'm not interested so much in concepts or messages or anything like that. I'm interested in creating emotions, and this script does that quite successfully, though it's an extremely difficult part for Joanne.'

Just how difficult it was, Woodward herself describes: 'When Paul was directing me in *Marigolds*, I came close to sheer insanity,' she admits. 'The role had an effect on me both during the shooting and afterwards. At home, I was a monster, and Paul and I avoided each other as much as possible,' she admits. 'There was something ugly about the character of Beatrice that got to me. Such putrefaction inside. I understood her all too well,' Joanne admits. 'You know, if you're rejected and you reject yourself, then the goodness gets swallowed up by the ugliness.'

Joanne makes it clear that, in spite of her problems with the role, her 'director' did not add to them. 'Being directed by my husband is not a problem,' she said. 'Paul is the easiest person in the world . . . I never have to explain myself to him like I do with directors I don't know.'

What was a taxing role for Joanne, and perhaps also a harder-than-usual directing shoot for Paul, had one distinct bright spot, and that was their daughter Nell.

'It's easy to direct her,' Paul said at the time. 'Her own quality carries. Her quality not as a performer, but as a person, carries her through. Put her face on camera and let her twitch away and you've got a scene.'

'Nell won't ever need a psychiatrist,' Joanne said about her first-born daughter. 'She's not an actress in the first place and couldn't care less about it in the second place. She loves the camaraderie of being part of a movie, and she loves the money because she has a whole menagerie to support and it was like getting an allowance. The only similarities between her and that child in the movie are her interests in science and her poetic outlook on life.

'She'd like to be an ornithologist,' Joanne went on. 'Her library is a huge compendium of books on hawks and eagles.

She owns every book ever written about pigeons. We gave her an electric handsaw for Christmas so she can build pigeon houses,' she said at the time of her surprising 13-year-old. 'I think she only acted in the film because Paul told her he refused to pay for her pigeon food anymore. Now the other kids want to know when they will get to be actors, too. I think they think it's always fun to go to work if Daddy is directing and Mommy is starring, but if they ever have to face the reality and toughness of the business, they'll change their minds,' Joanne said with what may have been more than a hint of wishful thinking.

What impact did *The Effect of Gamma Rays on Man-in-the-Moon Marigolds* have on the public? Well, the critics gave Newman points for excellent directing and Joanne Woodward points for effective acting, but the film was not a popular success. The subject matter was just too serious for the general public. Also, the title should definitely have been changed, or at least shortened, to make it more enticing for audiences.

There were many who felt that Joanne's acting job in *Marigolds* was Academy Award material and that she was passed over for a nomination unfairly. Others, while acknowledging Woodward's soaring talent as an acress, felt that since *Rachel, Rachel* she had not been offered the right roles. Woodward herself was inclined to agree. Moreover, she felt that as an actress in her early forties, plum roles were going to be even harder to get.

Not long after making *Marigolds*, however, Joanne tried once more for a bravura film role that would 'click' with her talents the same way *Eve* and *Rachel* had. She was heartened by the fact that Stewart Stern, an old family friend whose writing Joanne respected, had written the screenplay with her in mind. The film was initially entitled *Death of a Snow Queen*, then changed to *Souvenirs*, and finally to *Summer Wishes, Winter Dreams*, the title under which it was released.

In the film, Joanne plays a woman in her forties who is

going through a difficult time, to say the least. She and her husband (Martin Balsam) have grown so estranged that they aren't even on speaking terms. Then her mother dies of a heart attack as she looks on helplessly; her grown daughter rejects her, and her son turns out to be gay. But since the woman has been cold and emotionally isolated to all of these family members to begin with, one can hardly summon up sympathy for her.

But evidently Joanne Woodward did before she contracted to play the role. 'Stewart Stern, who wrote one of my favourite films, *Rachel, Rachel* for me, is also the author of this one,' she said while filming it, 'and it really is a beautiful script. It's about a woman who makes the awful discovery of how brief life really is, too brief even to correct one's worst mistakes, and even worse, too brief really to ever change,' Joanne said. 'It's very depressing,' she added, 'and just between you and me, I've just about had it with being depressed.'

Joanne's impatience during the shooting of *Summer Wishes, Winter Dreams* was obvious at one point when she challenged the director, saying: 'We'd better finish this picture by Friday, because I'm going off to Switzerland, period, after that.'

He was reported to have answered that there was no problem, because he had plans to go to Florida.

When an on-the-set interviewer asked Joanne what she did when she wasn't making films, her answer gives a rare and illuminating glimpse into this great actress' life. 'I go to class,' she said. 'I raise my family. I do needlework. I make attempts to play the guitar. I play the recorder. I go to the ballet. I work on whatever cause I'm involved in at the moment. I travel with my husband. Not very exciting actually,' she concluded.

When the interviewer (John Tallmer for the *New York Post*) asked what kind of classes Joanne attended, she answered, 'Ballet classes, in Connecticut. And I'm about to go back to the Center for Continuing Education at Sarah

Lawrence. I once went to college for two years; now I'm resuming ... Learning should be continuous anyway,' Joanne opined.

When Tallmer asked what she had been reading lately, Joanne said, very definitely keeping up her reputation as an intellectual: 'I've just finished the new biography of Isadora Duncan. I've just started the new book – Paul gave it to me – by Simone de Beauvoir. And I've just finished a marvellous project – I don't know what it's worth – all of Anthony Trollope. Literally for two years that's all I read, except for an occasional lapse into Agatha Christie,' Joanne admitted.

Even though *The Life and Times of Judge Roy Bean* had been a dismal failure, Newman teamed up again with director John Huston a year later. The film was *The Mackintosh Man*, an espionage 'thriller' which fell flat on its face at the box office.

At this point in his career, Newman was really 'hurtin' for a hit', and with the help of his famous luck, the right film came along at the right time – yet again. *The Sting* reunited the famous duo from *Butch Cassidy and the Sundance Kid*, this time as con artists rather than shoot-'em-up out-laws. Moreover, Newman and Redford were directed in this clever, fast-paced romp by the same director who had made Butch and the Kid famous – George Roy Hill.

The plot is circuitous and complicated, but the characters played by Newman and Redford – who unite in order to defraud an unscrupulous crime boss (played by Robert Shaw) out of a huge sum of money – manage to keep the viewer interested. This film is definitely of the style-over-content variety, depending heavily on the nostalgic 1930s crime-and-con-game mystique, as well as on the appeal of its two handsome, popular stars. The success of *The Sting*, with its slick style, was also owing to its musical score, which was made up of Scott Joplin piano rags. Marvin Hamlisch, who adapted them for use, however, came under fire. Many people said he shouldn't have used these tunes in a film set in a much later era than the one in which the music was composed.

However, purist type criticism aside, *The Sting* was a box office success, drawing fans of Redford and Newman who merely wanted a couple of hours' worth of snappy entertainment.

The following excerpt from a review in *Variety* says it all: '(*The Sting*) has all the signs of a blockbuster. Paul Newman and Robert Redford are superbly re-teamed. George Roy Hill's outstanding direction of David S. Ward's finely-crafted story of multiple deception and surprise ending will delight both mass and class audiences . . . the three stars make all the difference between simply a good story and a superior one. Newman, in a somewhat older role than normally, opens the door wide to another facet of his career; he rounds out his characterisation of an old pro making his last big score.'

The fact that Redford was nominated for an Academy Award for his work in *The Sting* while he wasn't, supposedly didn't bother Newman at all. 'After all,' he remarked to a friend, 'I've lost four of 'em already (for *Cat on a Hot Tin Roof, The Hustler, Hud* and *Cool Hand Luke*). Why should I want to be nominated and defeated a fifth time?'

Far from holding any grudge against Redford, Newman enjoyed working with him in both *Butch Cassidy* and *The Sting*. 'I'd welcome another opportunity to do a picture with Redford,' Paul said, 'but it would have to be something special, something as good or better than *The Sting*. I wish it would happen, because we have such a marvellous time on the set. I'm getting to that age now where it's extremely important for me to have fun while making films. Yes, Redford and I are good friends,' he reiterated, 'but the motion picture business is peculiar – you build very strong friendships for three or four months on a picture, then you don't see the guy for years.'

As it happened, even with a success like *The Sting* to his credit, Paul was finding that film offers weren't exactly pouring in.

'I'm the type of guy who can't lay off for a long time,' Paul said. 'It's physically and mentally important that I work steadily. I can't spend all my time racing cars ... Last February (1974) I desperately wanted to work, but I couldn't find anything to do.'

After a few more months of involuntary idleness, Newman agreed to play the part of the architect in *The Towering Inferno*. 'It's a distinguished film of its kind,' Paul said. 'There's nothing wrong with being in a movie loaded with star performers.'

Paul didn't even seem to mind that his role had been turned down by one of his co-stars, Steve McQueen. First Steve had wanted to portray the architect, but had later changed his mind and opted for the more dramatic and heroic fireman's role.

'It didn't matter to me what role I played,' Newman insisted. 'It didn't matter to me in the *Butch Cassidy* movie either. If Marlon Brando had been in the picture as was suggested at first, I would have played the Sundance Kid. If Warren Beatty had consented to do the picture, I would have played Butch. It didn't make any difference because they were both marvellous parts.'

The roles in *The Towering Inferno* were far from marvellous. The point was that Paul Newman was being paid close to $1 million per film appearance by this time, and in a movie like *The Towering Inferno* where there were lots of famous actors in supporting roles, it really was immaterial to Newman which part he played.

Paul was more concerned when his son Scott, then 25, who had a job as stuntman on the film, got trapped in a blaze on the *Inferno* set. Paul, who'd recommended Scott for the job, began to wish that his only son would find a safer occupation.

In 1975 Newman and Woodward were reunited on screen once again in *The Drowning Pool*, the film version of Ross MacDonald's mystery novel by the same name. In this film, Newman reprises his role as the private detective, Harper

(Archer in the original MacDonald novels). The film *Harper*, released almost ten years before in 1966, had been a big hit, and all concerned hoped that the popularity would carry over into *The Drowning Pool*, even though many years separated the two.

In *The Drowning Pool*, Joanne plays Mavis, an ex-lover of Harper's. She has since married and has consulted Harper to find out who is threatening to expose her current illicit love affair. Besides the character played by his wife, there is no dearth of other female co-stars in the movie, including Coral Browne, Gail Strickland, Melanie Griffith and Linda Haynes. Tony Franciosa is featured as a police chief and Murray Hamilton as an oil-developer villain.

For some reason, the setting of *The Drowning Pool* was shifted from Southern California (where all the Lew Archer stories are set) to New Orleans. This locale, while picturesque, did not make much sense in terms of the plot – conservationists versus oil interests – and elicited some criticism.

As a whole, *The Drowning Pool* was not a critical success. The plot didn't ring true, and more than one reviewer found Newman's depiction of Harper this time to be less than convincing.

'As Harper in New Orleans, Newman is tough and sassy,' Molly Haskell wrote in *The Village Voice*. 'The screenplay . . . gives him the best of it in smart rejoinders, but it is the smart talk of an adolescent who knows nothing can happen to him, not that of a grown man forestalling fear. The vulnerability, the emotional 'fall' by which the detective in some ways atones for the destruction his very presence precipitates, is missing in Harper.

'Newman is too much the Beautiful Person, too little the battered figure who has seen, and added his own signature to, the seamy side of life,' Haskell wrote. '. . . Newman can let his hair go grey, can grow a five o'clock shadow, can lose a button from his button-down shirt, can get bloodied up, and he still seems to be wearing a surgical mask and rubber gloves over that part of him that might be touched by contact with another person.

'This emotional fastidiousness becomes unpleasant as in *The Drowning Pool* he is constantly besieged by beautiful women whom he rejects with all the regret one would lavish on unappetising flavours of ice cream,' she concluded.

Newman himself couldn't help but agree with the critics on this one. 'It's the only time I ever played the same character twice, and it didn't work,' he admitted.

Perhaps part of the reason the *Harper* sequel didn't work was the very fact that it was a repeat role for Newman and therefore was boring for him. At this point, Paul Newman was pretty bored with his screen career in general. It had been quite some time since he'd been offered a role which was challenging to him personally.

Right after making *The Towering Inferno* and *The Drowning Pool*, Paul said to a reviewer, 'I'm prepared to work in any category, if the work is distinguished. Only two things I won't do – something pornographic or violent.' However, he added, 'I don't know if I'm anxious to do another film as an actor – except for *Buffalo Bill and the Indians*.'

This upcoming project was a collaboration between Newman and his new friend and colleague, Robert Altman, who had become famous for his eclectic, off-beat style of movie direction. Some called him a genius, some a fool or worse, but Altman had attracted lots of attention through films such as *Three Women*, *Nashville* and *The Wedding*. Soon after meeting him, Newman fell under his spell, and before long the two became great friends. Paul's oldest daughter, Susan, later obtained a part in *The Wedding*.

When Newman and Altman decided they wanted to work on a film together, Paul showed him a play, *Indians*, by Arthur Kopit, which the Newman-Forman partnership had purchased rights to way back in 1969. Newman and Altman set to work with other writers, developing the play into a movie script. By the time they were finished, the script bore little resemblance to the original play. It was the idea of *Indians* that excited Altman and Newman – exposing the myths that surround Buffalo Bill as a hero and the Indians as the bad guys. As a working title for their proposed film, Newman and Altman chose the ungainly *'Buffalo Bill and the Indians, or Sitting Bull's History Lesson.'*

Even though the title was later shortened, the film turned out to be two hours long. Both the script and the story were jumbled, and critics branded the movie as virtually incoherent. Newman's depiction of Buffalo Bill received praise, but it was not enough to save the film, which was a major disaster.

That same year, and in Paul's same adventurous quest to find film roles that were new and challenging, he took a small part in Mel Brooks' zany comedy, *Silent Movie*. The film was full of similar appearances by other stars and Newman's part was completely without dialogue, a definite 'first' for him.

In still another film made in 1977, Newman found a challenge and a change of pace playing a cantankerous, ageing ice hockey coach who is trying to come to grips with his uncertain future and the prospect of old age. The film, *Slap Shot*, is not only entertaining, but exciting too, due in part to its actual ice hockey sequences. The movie also became known, if not notorious, for its generous use of foul language.

'One of my favourite movies,' Newman said of *Slap Shot*. 'Unfortunately, that character is a lot closer to me than I would care to admit – vulgar, on the skids,' he said jokingly.

'It may not have been the best movie I ever made, but it was the most original role I'd played in years,' Paul told an interviewer. 'The funny thing is, when I did it I knew I'd make a lot of enemies. I got one letter from a woman in Indianapolis who said I raced at *her* track in 1968 (for *Winning*) and that this was the high point of her life. 'But last night I saw *Slap Shot*,' she wrote, 'and if you ever set foot on my property, I'll set the dogs on you!'

The critics gave Newman winning points for his role in *Slap Shot*, foul language and all, and the film did fairly well at the box office. In retrospect, Paul's role as the ageing ice hockey coach can be seen as one of his first as a character actor. While this was inevitable for Newman, over 50 at this point, it also turned out to be a boon for him as an actor. Before, Newman's breath-taking good looks had sometimes got in the way of his reputation as an actor of breadth and scope.

Slap Shot represented an exception, but by and large Paul Newman was discouraged by the spate of poor roles in even poorer films which had been his lot for most of the 1970s. As it was to turn out, this period represented a fallow period between his early years as a handsome matinee idol and his later years as a vastly talented and still handsome character actor. But at the time Newman was so disillusioned about his film career that he almost abandoned it completely in favour of his passionate interest in sports car racing.

As mentioned, Paul first got interested in the sport during the filming of *Winning* in 1968. From the start, it filled in a lot of gaps in his life.

'I always wanted to be an athlete, a football player or a basketball player,' he said. 'I tried skiing for ten years. The only thing I ever felt graceful at was racing a car, and that took me ten years to learn.'

Racing was not only a test of skill and a new learning experience – it was also a way for Paul to escape the rigours of being a world-famous film star. Wearing a helmet emblazoned only with the initials 'P.L.N.', he could enjoy a sense of freedom and anonymity sealed up in a sleek, slick Ferrari or Porsche as he raced at high speeds around various tracks on the amateur circuit. Racing was a welcome change from movie making, in that it took place in the here and now. Paul was asked to 'show his stuff' during a set amount of time, and he knew the results of his competition as soon as the race was over. Unlike movie making, the project didn't drag on for months, subject to a thousand different conditions and delays.

In 1977, Newman had spent almost five years on the amateur driving circuit and had done spectacularly well, especially considering that he had only become involved with the sport in his late forties. In the autumn of 1976, Paul was awarded the President's Cup, the highest amateur trophy for the Sports Car Club of America, and at least twice he was to prove the national champion in his class.

As an example of Newman's prowess, at the 24-hour endurance race at Daytona, Florida, in the spring of 1977, Newman and his more experienced team-mates, Milt Minter and Elliott Forbes-Robinson, came in fifth, just 50 laps behind the winner. 57 cars had started and only 24 finished. Newman drove a total of six and a half hours, half of them at night.

'I'd never driven at night before,' Paul said after the race. 'I'd never driven a car with this much horsepower and I'd never been involved in a race more than three or four hours long. Would I like to do it again? You bet your life!'

'He's very dedicated,' said Forbes-Robinson. 'I don't think there are many people who could start driving competitively at the age Paul did and be doing anywhere near as well.'

Paul's technique of calming his nerves and preparing himself before the race amazed his two teammates. He shut himself up in his trailer and listened to tapes of Bach and Beethoven while visualising every twist and turn in the track in his mind's eye.

'There's just no Hollywood about him,' Minter said. 'And he's smart. You tell him about a driving mistake and it's the last time he'll make it.'

Shortly after this particular race was over, Paul made arrangements to fly to London, where Joanne was shooting a film for British television. Her co-star happened to be one of the world's most gifted actors – Sir Laurence Olivier.

Chapter 9

A midlife crisis in terms of being a film star had hit Joanne Woodward in the early 1970s also. Rarely offered starring roles because of Hollywood's hang-up with youthfulness, Joanne found herself in a double-edged trap. Not only did she seem relegated to playing menopausal types who were unsympathetic at best and half-psychotic at worst, but she also felt that her career was becoming too tied in with her husband's.

After completing *The Drowning Pool* in 1975, Joanne said, 'It would be very difficult for me to do another movie – particularly one with Paul. I have to do something that's mine, not as an appendage.'

Joanne went on to make this resolution of hers a reality. She put out feelers and found that there were still opportunities available to her as an actress and she didn't have to settle for roles that weren't fulfilling to her personally. Quality productions both on TV and in movies soon began to open to Joanne Woodward.

Joanne's 'renaissance' began with an excellent TV production of *Sybil*, with Woodward in the role of the psychiatrist and Sally Field playing the patient who turned out to have 16 different personalities.

Another small role in a film which she greatly enjoyed was when Joanne played Gelsey Kirkland's mother in the highly praised film about ballet, *The Turning Point*.

And in the spring of 1977, while her husband competed in the Daytona endurance race, Joanne had the honour and pleasure of co-starring with Sir Laurence Olivier, in William Inge's play, *Come Back, Little Sheba*. Also featured was another American actress, young Carrie Fisher, daughter of Debbie Reynolds and Eddie Fisher.

Later that year, Joanne found herself back in Hollywood on the set of Burt Reynold's black comedy, *The End*, in which Woodward had a featured role, her first in quite some time. She found it enjoyable to work with Reynolds, who both acted in and directed the film; nevertheless, being back on a Hollywood set was quite a transition for Joanne.

'What I've gone through is a normal phenomenon, particularly with women of my age,' Woodward told an interviewer. 'We were raised in a certain way, that you were supposed to stay home with your children. Then in the middle of our staying home we were suddenly told, "No, you must get out and free yourself." We had six children between the two of us,' she went on, 'so it was very difficult.'

Then, in a surprising statement, the actress said, 'I do hope my children understand that although I'm second to none in my adoration for them, I would not have had children had I to do it all over again.' Even more surprisingly, Joanne said, 'I probably wouldn't get married, either. I think actors, generally speaking, don't make very good parents. My tendency is to shriek and throw things, being childish myself, as most actors are.

'And, being a total actress − I really like to act morning, noon and night − that was another problem our girls had to suffer with because not always being allowed to act on stage or screen, I was giving brilliant performances at home,' Joanne admitted.

In this instance it seems that Joanne Woodward is being too hard on herself, a tendency to which she is prone.

Her statement that if she had it to do all over again she probably wouldn't have children, really should be understood as meaning that when she was young, women didn't really have a choice. It was taken for granted that every woman should get married, have children and devote her life to those children.

In terms of her own daughters, Joanne wants to make sure that they do have an option. 'What I mean when I say I'm raising my children not to have children is that this should not be their sole aim in life,' she told Kay Gardella in an interview. 'Getting married and having children isn't why you grow up. You grow up to become a human being first . . . what I sincerely don't want is for my girls to feel that that is all there is to life and if they don't get married and have children they're unfulfilled,' she explained.

As for Joanne, she felt that she really only had a chance to fulfil herself as a human being in her late forties, after her daughters were almost grown. During the years that she was mainly confined to home, it was her newfound and passionate interest in ballet – both taking lessons herself and attending performances – that gave Joanne a sense of creativity.

Having discovered ballet too late in life to become a performer herself, Joanne did the next best thing. 'I feel creative,' she said. 'I've done the only thing I could – provide the money.'

At first Joanne helped many different ballet groups, drawing money from the No Sutch Foundation, which she and Paul had set up to help various charities and causes. 'We each have our own thing,' Joanne said of herself and Paul. 'He has his racing. I go to the ballet. He is a very good financial supporter,' she acknowledged. 'I hate to ask, but when the chips are down, Paul comes through.'

Joanne's interest in ballet became focused on one troupe in particular, called Dancers. Conceived by former American Ballet Theatre soloist Dennis Wayne, Dancers is an experimental ensemble which is designed to promote the individual dancer. Both Wayne and Woodward felt that all too many talented performers were being lost in the shuffle of the major, star-oriented dance companies.

In 1975, Dennis Wayne invited Joanne to become chairman of the board of Dancers, and ever since then she has been tireless in her efforts to raise money for the group. Supporting Dancers has had a beneficial effect on Joanne's acting career, spurring her on to look for projects that she will enjoy and that will pay well – so that she can donate her earnings to Dancers.

'I do what I like to do now, which is to act,' Joanne said on the set of *The End*, 'and that does not necessarily mean in movies. But when I do act in movies, I do it mostly for the money because it's very expensive supporting a ballet company.'

In the autumn of 1977 Joanne had an opportunity to work extra hard as an actress when she agreed to portray a housewife-turned-Marathon runner in the CBS-TV special, *See How She Runs*. The film, which takes place in Boston, is a story of a 40-year-old schoolteacher who, after her divorce, has to raise two daughters on her own. Lissie Newman, then 16, played one of the daughters, while young actress Mary Beth Manning played the other. Stuck in the rut of her never-ending responsibilities, Joanne's character, Betty Quinn, takes up jogging as a diversion. This hobby becomes an obsession, and Betty ends up running in the 26-mile Boston Marathon.

Joanne ended up becoming quite an accomplished runner herself. She started out by jogging up to three miles a day for three months, and then worked up gradually into running. 'Running is great fun,' she said gamely. 'Besides, it's good for the behind.'

During the actual filming of *See How She Runs*, Joanne would sometimes put in four to six miles per day for the cameras, before 'collapsing' at the Somerville Holiday Inn outside Boston, where Paul, Lissie, and their youngest daughter, Clea, then 12, were also staying. The special, which was shown early in 1978, was well received.

That same spring, Paul Newman received an honour which was as unexpected as it was gratifying. He was asked to be one of three citizen delegates to a special session of the United Nations General Assembly. The topic to be discussed was nuclear disarmament, one of Newman's strongest political beliefs. Even so, Paul felt overawed at the prospect at first and was going to decline.

'Then I figured that most people in the United States knew little about the arms race,' he said. 'I gave the offer some very serious thought and agreed.' Another reason Paul decided to do his civic duty was 'because I don't want my children to write on my tombstone that here lies a lazy old man who was never part of his time. It is part of our time to work for disarmament,' he said.

Paul took his appointment seriously. He put in full days at the U.N. from the time he was appointed in May until the special session ended on July 1st. After a debate on the pros and cons of nuclear disarmament, the delegates agreed on a vague document which proposed future disarmament negotiations.

During the debate and meeting, Newman made many intelligent and hard-hitting remarks. 'Communicating the substance of these arms proposals isn't easy,' he said. 'It's perhaps the hardest job I've ever had.'

Yet, during the conference, Newman made his points with both wit and humour. For example, he told the following little story: 'Do you know the story of the airline pilot who told his passengers, "I've got some good news and some bad news. First the bad news. We are hopelessly lost. Now the good news. We're making wonderful time." That's the message,' Paul concluded.

Being thought of highly enough to be appointed as a citizen delegate at the U.N. was one of the peak experiences of Paul Newman's life. Unfortunately, near the end of that same year, one of the worst experiences of his life took place. That was the tragic death of Newman's first-born child and only son, Scott, at the age of 28.

Scott's tragic death was caused by an accidental overdose of drugs and alcohol. Unfortunately, Scott had been having problems for some time and his death was not completely unexpected, at least by Paul. Aware of his son's psychological instability and chronic drug usage, Newman had told several close friends that he lived in fear of a telephone call in the middle of the night telling him that something terrible had happened to his son.

When the call actually came, on November 19, 1978, Paul was at his alma mater, Kenyon College, in Ohio. Paul had taken time out of his busy schedule to go there and direct a group of drama students in a new play by Michael Cristofer called *C.C.Pyle and the Bunion Derby*.

In shock and stranded on campus until the next day, it is said that Newman called his young cast members together, told them the tragic news, and then added, 'It would help me if you'd all be as rowdy as possible.' Soon after, they showed up in Newman's room wearing clownish clothes, bearing a case of beer and a bottle of Scotch. According to campus legend, Newman took a deep swig of the whisky and confided to his visitors that 'It's the first time I've touched hard stuff in eight years.' Then, he supposedly gently bade his guests goodnight and shut himself in for what must surely have been one of the most painful and loneliest nights of his life.

The funeral, which took place in California, was attended by only the immediate family: Jacqueline Witte Robinson, Scott's mother, and her husband; Susan and Stephanie, Scott's sisters; and naturally Paul; Joanne, his stepmother; and Nell, Lissie and Clea, his half-sisters. As with the death of any young person, the survivors' feelings of grief and loss were compounded by the sense of needless waste.

Scott Newman's death was hard on every member of his family. For the five sisters it represented the ugly, unsettling intrusion of death into their young lives, claiming a beloved brother who was also a contemporary. For Scott's mother, Jackie, as well as his father, Paul, it represented the death of not only their first-born child, but also their only son. For Joanne Woodward, who had stepmothered Scott for a good part of every year since the boy was seven, the shock and grief were intense also.

Even though Scott's death was ruled by the coroner as 'accidental', the alcohol and drugs he took on that last fatal day were self-administered and it had been Scott's emotional turmoil which had driven him to overindulge. For any parent whose child dies this way, it is almost inevitable to ask, 'Why?' and even more wrenchingly, to wonder, 'Where did I go wrong?'

Paul Newman was no exception. He couldn't help but think back to the early years of Scott's childhood when he had been married to Jackie. They had been years of struggle, but there had been happiness, too. Sadly, as Paul's career took off, the marriage began to disintegrate, due mainly to his being away from home so much of the time. Then his love affair with Joanne Woodward had started, eventually causing his first marriage to end.

There is evidence to suggest that Scott Newman was nervous and highly-strung from the start. A close friend of Paul and Jackie's remembers going to their apartment when Scott was two and 'being unable to carry on a conversation because he was yelling and screaming. He was uncontrollable.'

Scott may well have been hyperactive, a condition which was not as readily recognised and treated then as it is today. At any rate, while many two-year-olds have tantrums and then outgrow them, Scott's temper grew even more ungovernable as time went on.

'Scott suffered the most from his father's frequent absences from home,' another friend of the family said. 'Maybe being the only boy and being the oldest had something to do with it, but I think it was mostly because he was the most sensitive. When Paul was around, I remember Scott's tantrums being even worse. Perhaps this was his way of trying to get attention from his father. Then again, I feel the boy was also responding to tensions between Paul and Jackie. Kids know when their parents are having problems, especially a sensitive kid like Scott.'

There were other pressures to follow: the break-up of his parents' marriage, his father's remarriage to Joanne Woodward; his mother's move to California with Scott and his sisters, and then her own remarriage.

Both Jackie and Paul did their best to make these changes as easy as possible for their children, whom they dearly loved. But the truth is, the divorce and subsequent remarriage of both parents never can be easy on a child, and Scott took the events hardest of all.

Scott, Susan and Stephanie were always welcome at the Newmans' home, whether they were in Connecticut or California, and always spent a good part of their summer with their father and stepmother. Joanne worked especially hard to make the children feel loved and at home. Newman's oldest three kids were always included at special parties and premieres having to do with Paul's film career. In photographs, Joanne is shown just as often with her arm around Susan or Stephanie as she is embracing her own daughters. Scott is noticeably absent from these photos, which is significant, since he was surely invited. But from the start he held back from the family warmth offered by his father and Joanne. When he did stay with them, he was described as 'a disruptive influence' by more than one family friend.

When Scott entered his teen years, the clashes with his father became even worse. When the boy was visiting Paul and Joanne, fights between father and son would often be so heated that outright violence was feared by Joanne and the girls. Many of the fights had to do with money. Paul had always fought the idea of his kids growing up as over-privileged 'Hollywood brats'. Indeed, that's one reason why he and Joanne made their home in Westport, Connecticut. While he sent Scott to the best private schools, Paul didn't believe in buying his kids everything they wanted and giving them huge allowances. Instead of seeing this as a reflection of his father's heartfelt inner values, Scott chose to take what he perceived as Paul's 'stinginess' as another form of rejection. All along he had somehow felt 'cheated' by his father – because Paul had split up with his mother and remarried, and because his father was rich and famous and a movie star. Like so many sons, Scott felt obliged to 'compete' with his father, and yet he knew that to surpass or even come close to his father's success was next to impossible.

Joanne tried to smooth out the relations between her husband and his son – to no avail. She had tried to get through to the troubled teenager, only to be rebuffed rudely. According to insiders, Scott also took his resentment out on Joanne, to the point where the two of them would go months without speaking.

In the meantime, Scott just kept getting into trouble and being expelled from one expensive school after another. He managed to get accepted to college, but dropped out after less than two years.

At the age of 19, Scott was living on his own. He took up the first of the dangerous occupations he was to seek out – sky diving. Scott showed remarkable skill at this dangerous sport, soon qualifying as an instructor. He even taught parachuting to cadets at the United States Naval Academy.

Unfortunately, Scott took up another dangerous habit around this time – drinking. Driven to drink by the painful and uncontrollable emotions inside him, he often became violent when intoxicated. One of these incidents, which took place in 1974 while Scott was on a skiing holiday in the California Sierras, was serious enough to make the papers.

While out drinking, Scott got into a brawl. It took three local policemen to separate the six-foot, 180-pounder from the fracas and pile him into a police car. Even then, presumably in hand-cuffs, Scott continued to fight, kicking one of the officers in the head and causing the police car to run into a snow drift.

Scott was booked for felonious assault with a weapon and thrown into jail. Later he said sardonically, (and who could blame him) that 'the weapon was a boot'.

Paul Newman came to help his son. After a preliminary hearing, the charge was reduced to a misdemeanour, and eventually Scott got off with two years' probation and a $1,000 fine, which his father paid. It's said that Scott Newman deeply resented having to turn to his father for help. However, one hopes that Paul Newman didn't add to his son's shame by being too harsh on him. After all, Paul had had his own problems with drinking and his own run-ins with the law, and hopefully he was able to show some compassion and understanding to his similarly troubled son.

There is evidence that Paul did show such compassion. At any rate, it was round this time that Scott, through his father's influence, obtained a small role and some work as a stuntman in *The Towering Inferno*. However, as much as Scott yearned to make a name for himself in the movies as his father had, he wanted to do it on his own, without Paul's help.

When Scott heard that George Roy Hill (his father's close friend ever since Hill directed him in *Butch Cassidy* and later in *The Sting*) was doing a film about barn-storming aviators, he called and asked for work as a parachutist and stuntman. Of course, the film was the *The Great Waldo Pepper*, and Scott Newman was promptly hired.

'But did I get the job because I'm good – or because I'm Paul Newman's son?' Scott tormented himself and his friends with questions like this.

He continued to blame his father for all his problems, and at the same time he continued to seek work in show business. He managed to get small roles here and there both in movies and TV. He even tried singing in small nightclubs, billing himself as 'William Scott' to escape the family name, which poor, tormented Scott desperately admired and vehemently hated at the same time.

In between jobs, Scott continued to drown his sorrows in alcohol. Even more alarmingly, he now dabbled in whatever drugs he could get his hands on, either buying them illegally or cadging them from friends.

Paul knew that his son was in trouble, and he tried once again to reach out to him. This time Paul tried to interest Scott in his own growing passion for sports car racing on the amateur circuit. Knowing Scott's penchant for dangerous sports, Newman hoped that he would come to share his own love for fast cars. Scott did attend a few races and even tried his hand behind the wheel as a driver. But here again he was stymied by what was perhaps his fatal flaw – he resented his father's skill at the sport and felt too overshadowed by him to dare to compete.

So, Paul, who can never be accused of being an uncaring father, no matter what his own son thought, tried to help Scott in the only way he knew how – by seeking professional help for him. First Paul hired Dr. Robert Scott of the Advanced Health Center of Newport Beach, California, to help Scott with his alcohol dependency problem.

Dr. Scott later said that 'Scott was terrorised by the idea of trying to be a professional actor. The risk of failure scared the hell out of him, so he relied on drugs and alcohol.'

When the alcohol treatment programme didn't work, Paul sought out various psychiatrists and psychologists for Scott, hoping one of them would be able to get through to the young man and relieve him of his anxieties, as well as his need for alcohol and drugs. Paul himself participated in these sessions, only to have his son end up blaming him for all his problems.

Still, Paul didn't give up. He finally settled on a clinical psychologist, Dr. Mark Weinstean, and his associate, Scott Steinberg, to be on call for Scott in times of stress. Dr.Weinstein agreed to provide therapy sessions whenever Scott needed them, and Steinberg would act as more of a caretaker, spending time with young Newman whenever the emotional stress got really bad.

But on the day of November 19, 1978, even Scott's psychological caretakers couldn't keep him from his ultimate self-destructive booze and drug trip. In fact, according to *Heartbreak Kids: The Tragedy of Hollywood's Children* by Bob Thomas, in which the following sequence of events is given, Scott's doctor even provided one of the prescription drugs which ended up contributing to his death – only because he mixed it with so many other substances.

'On the afternoon of Nov 19, 1978, Alan Scott Newman complained of pains in his chest and side. This time he attributed the cause to a motorcycle accident he had suffered a few weeks before,' Bob Thomas writes in *Heartbreak Kids*.

'Scott always seemed to have some kind of pain,' the narrative continues. 'He was a broad-shouldered, muscular six-footer, and in his 28 years he had led a physical life. He had always taken chances, whether parachuting from airplanes, as he had done 500 times, or practising movie stunts by falling off horses or tumbling down stairs.

'When he felt pain in his bones and muscles, he sought help from booze and drugs,' Thomas goes on. 'He sought the same relief when he underwent emotional stress, which was often.'

At around two in the afternoon on that fatal day, Scott went to a friend's apartment. It was Sunday, and the two watched a football game while drinking rum and cokes. Scott complained of pains behind his shoulder and under his ribs, and his friend offered him some Valium tablets. Whatever dosage they were, Scott supposedly took five immediately and three more an hour later.

Then, Scott and his friend (not named in *Heartbreak Kids*) went together to visit Dr. Mark Weinstein. According to author Bob Thomas, 'For an hour the young man told of his failure to find a career for himself and of his conflict with his father and his stepmother, Joanne Woodward.

'At the end of the session, Dr. Weinstein gave Scott a small sample bottle of painkiller Darvon,' Thomas continues.

After the therapy session, Scott and his friend, also accompanied by Scott's caretaker, Scott Steinberg, returned to the friend's apartment, where they drank more rum.

'Later in the evening, Steinberg accompanied Scott to his room at the Ramada Inn in Beverly Hills,' Thomas states. 'They chatted for a time, then Scott went to the bathroom and unknown to Steinberg, took some Quaaludes and cocaine. He soon became drowsy and went to bed at ten. He began snoring loudly.

'At eleven-thirty the snoring stopped. So did Scott's breathing. Paramedics rushed him to the New Hospital, where he was pronounced dead on arrival.'

If this account is accurate, and it seems to be, then Scott Newman, in the space of just nine hours, had ingested Valium, Darvon, Quaaludes and cocaine, as well as a large quantity of rum, into his system. Whereas to a normal person this seems like an enormous and perhaps even suicidal amount of substances, to a chronic drug abuser it would be 'all in a day's work'. In other words, Scott had probably taken this many drugs mixed with alcohol plenty of times in the past. He had just not counted on his body giving out, since it had always been able to handle whatever he put into it before.

Then again, while he had been anxious enough to require the services of his clinical psychologist and his associate, Scott Newman's mood on November 19th was no worse – and probably better – than it had been many times before. So, while the amount of drugs and alcohol in Scott Newman's system certainly was enough to kill him – and did – the death was ruled as 'accidental'.

The sense of grief and loss, and also waste, which Scott's whole family felt at his untimely death was shared also by his friends and by all the therapists who tried so hard to reach him and help him deal with his problems. No doubt Scott's parents, Paul Newman and Jackie Witte Robinson, suffered the most severe bereavement. Perhaps that is why Joanne

Woodward was the only one who spoke out openly about Scott and the tragic circumstances not only of his death, but his life.

'Scott was a bright kid,' Joanne told an interviewer in 1980, two years after his death, 'and maybe if he had known early on (about the dangers of drugs) he wouldn't have started.

'You have to do a positive thing for kids,' she went on. 'Negative things like throwing them in jail or sending them somewhere to be dried out won't work. What happened to Scott could have happened a lot of other times much earlier,' she admitted. 'We knew it and we have had to live with it.'

Then, with incredible courage, Joanne went on to tell the interviewer (and in effect the public) that her and Paul's oldest daughter, Nell, had also had a brush with drugs. 'She never got to the addict stage,' Joanne said, 'but what she did was to screw up in school and everything else in her life so that at age 21 she found herself way behind her peers.'

Fortunately, Nell's involvement with drugs was brief. With her parents' help, she got back on track and buckled down to her studies, intent on making her lifetime dream of being an ornithologist come true.

The nightmare of drug abuse among young people hit Paul and Joanne so close to home and so tragically that they decided to try and do something about it. As a tribute to the son they had loved dearly but hadn't been able to help, the Newmans set up the Scott Newman Foundation at the University of Southern California in Pasadena. The purpose of the Foundation is to provide information about the dangers of drugs to secondary school-age children in the hope that it will prevent future tragedies like the one that befell Scott. Paul's oldest daughter, Susan, runs the foundation.

'This may sound corny,' Joanne said, 'but we just didn't want Scott to have lived in vain.'

In an effort to cope with his grief (which he kept to himself in typical Newman fashion), Paul threw himself into work. In 1979, in spite of the disastrous *Buffalo Bill and the*

Indians, he teamed up again with director Robert Altman. This time the film was *Quintet*, a science fiction piece set in the Ice Age. The film was so poorly received by the critics that it came and went in a matter of weeks, with very few people ever seeing it.

Right after *Quintet*, Newman appeared in Irwin Allen's *When Time Ran Out*, a disaster film about volcanoes. Paul had hoped it would be 'a big commercial film', but instead it was 'a terrible mistake'. Even a good supporting cast which included William Holden and Jacqueline Bisset, couldn't help this film. It was a disaster, all right – at the box office.

'I made a couple of really bad ones back to back,' Paul said ruefully about these two films. Still, given the fact of his son's death and Paul's need to keep busy, any poor judgment he showed in taking them on is surely understandable.

Paul once again turned to directing at this point. 'I'm more selective about what I direct than about what I act in,' Newman admitted. And even though the project was for television, he generated it himself. The play was *The Shadow Box*, for which Michael Cristofer won the Pulitzer Prize. Although it's a work about terminal cancer patients, it is in no way depressing. Paul said that he chose it because 'it says we should *use* our time, not wait until tomorrow or until we are facing death, but use it today. If there's anything I'm interested in in this anaesthetised society, it's emotion,' he continued. 'I want to really get to an audience and wake them up.'

Meantime, Paul's accomplishments in his 'other' career, sports car racing, had shaken up not only the United States but Europe, too. Many believed that Newman was crazy to enter the famous Le Mans race in 1979. At age 54 he was the oldest driver in the notoriously tough 24-hour-long race, in which 18 drivers had died since its inception. But Paul insisted upon taking the challenge, alternating with his two co-drivers in guiding their red Porsche 935 Twin Turbo around the rain-slicked course.

Out of 55 entries, 33 were unable to finish the race. As the race progressed it became clear that almost anything could happen. For a while it seemed that Newman and his team had the race in the bag when the front-running Porsche stalled. But then Paul's car lost 18 precious minutes in a pit stop that should have taken 30 seconds, because of a 'seized wheel nut'. They squeaked into a second place win in the nick of time after their car started spewing oil, a considerable victory indeed. With silver cup in hand, Paul put through a trans-Atlantic call to Joanne. She was watching another Newman competitor that day – their youngest daughter Clea who was in a horse show.

Needless to say, Paul was thrilled at his victory, even if it was second place. Newman's teammates and friends on the racing circuit were unanimous in their praise and support of him. 'He's not just good – he's a tremendous driver,' driver Dick Barbour said.

And according to Lime Rock boss Jim Haynes, 'If he (Paul) had started in his twenties, there is no doubt he would be a world champion.'

In addition to racing, Newman ranks top in two other categories – barbecuing great hamburgers and perpetrating great pranks. One time he had competitor Bob Tullius' logo painted upside down on the side of a garbage truck and then had it sent around the track. He followed this up with a banner, towed by an aeroplane that read, 'Tullius Gobbles'. To get back at him, Tullius talked some Georgia cops into pulling Newman over and detaining him for 'impersonating an actor'.

Along the same lines, Newman and Redford have been pulling pranks on each other ever since their *Butch Cassidy and the Sundance Kid* days. One time Redford sent Newman a totally demolished Porsche for his birthday. Paul retaliated by sending the same Porsche back to Bob – after he had it compacted into a foot-square cube. This he had placed in the middle of Redford's living room, like a piece of sculpture. To keep Newman from enjoying the satisfaction of this stroke of prankster genius, neither Redford or any of his family members ever mentioned the mysterious metal cube, acting as if the incident had never happened.

In the autumn of 1979, Joanne was back in Hollywood, on location for another CBS-TV special, *The Streets of L.A.*. The producer, George Englund and the writer, Marvin Gluck, were the same team Joanne had worked with on *See How She Runs*, and she was pleased about the reunion. This time the story was based on a true incident involving a Los Angeles woman, Janice Berger, who, upon coming home one evening to find the tyres of her new car slashed, decided to do something about it on her own.

In the story as adapted for TV, the woman Joanne played has come to California hoping to make a fresh start after both her marriage and her life fall apart. 'Then these young Chicano men slash her tyres and push her over the edge,' Woodward explained. 'She simply has to confront them. She's terribly angry because everything is messed up in her life. But she finds that they're angry too, for many of the same reasons. And so the experience is traumatic – a total culture shock – for them all.'

After talking to a interviewer about her role in *The Streets of L.A.*, Joanne talked a bit about her personal life, which is a rarity for her. 'If it's strictly about work I'm involved in, that's one thing,' Joanne said. 'But simply to do a personal interview doesn't make much sense to me, because I don't think actors should talk about acting, and I don't have anything else to say that is particularly interesting.'

Perhaps the interviewer, Joseph N. Bell from *The Christian Science Monitor* managed to convince Woodward that, on the contrary, many people consider almost anything she has to say interesting, because they admire her as both an actress and a person.

One thing Joanne was usually willing to talk about was Dancers, the company she helped fund. 'The company is having its ups and downs,' she told Bell. 'As to whether or not it will survive, I don't know. The possibility of survival of any art form in this country – but especially ballet and opera – is very low because there is little or no government involvement.

'The closest I ever got to politics was serving on the dance panel of the National Endowment of Arts for three years, and it came as a real shock . . . (to) realise that the Pentagon spends more in one day than the government gives to the arts in a year,' Woodward went on. 'We're the only country in the world, you know, in which that is true . . . There's nothing very similar about England and Russia, for example, except that both of them fully support their arts. Why do we have to be different? We've got more money than anybody,' she wondered aloud.

Getting around to more personal subjects, Joanne spoke about fame and how it affected her life and Paul's. In terms of being bothered by the public, Joanne said, 'I've never had much of a problem with that because I'm not easily recognised. I tend to look different in every film I do, so there's no image to fasten on.'

Paul was the one who suffered from constantly being chased by fans, she went on '. . . because he's as recognisable as Mount Rushmore. He can't avoid it, and that can be bothersome, but a funny thing has happened as we've got older: We've sort of tended to become elder statesmen, and people treat us in that way. It's nice,' Joanne commented, 'I really like it. People are very kind. I guess it's when they stop grabbing at you and want, instead, to talk about things you've done – in a good way.'

As with most celebrities, Joanne said that she and Paul suffer from being misquoted and having outright lies spread about them.

'Take Paul's racing, for example,' she said. 'I'm constantly quoted as saying that I'm terrified about it and hate to see him race. That's simply not true. I'm at every race I can possibly get to, and I love it. It's an interesting sport for a grown man who's doing what he chooses to do.'

In the same way, Joanne pointed out, the reporters said that Paul never went to the ballet. 'He does go,' she contradicted. 'He obviously doesn't enjoy ballet as much as I do, nor do I enjoy racing as much as he does, but on the other hand, we do share. But the myths go on.'

Some of the myths perpetuated about the Newmans are a lot more damaging and sensational than whether he likes ballet and she likes sports car racing. Some of the most prevalent of these are about Paul and Joanne's marriage. One rumour has it that it's strictly a 'marriage of convenience', while another says that it's a union that runs rampant with sexual perversions.

When one interviewer brought up these stories to Joanne, the actress threw up her hands and began to laugh wildly. 'It's all true,' she said, pretending the game was up. 'It's a marriage of convenience and we are sex maniacs and everything in between. I think it makes it so much more interesting. The children, too – Nell, Lissie, Clea – all nymphomaniacs,' Joanne went on sarcastically. 'And don't forget the chicken and the skunk,' she added, referring to her children's assortment of wildlife at their home in Connecticut.

The main point about the Newman marriage is that it has survived and is still surviving into its third decade. Of course it hasn't always been easy. 'Joanne and I have had difficult, body bending confrontations, but we haven't surrendered,' Paul said. 'I've packed up and left a few times, and then I realise I have no place to go and I'm back in ten minutes. Ultimately, I think we both delight in watching the progression. And we laugh a lot,' he added.

As in any enduring marriage, both the Newmans have had to work hard at keeping it together. Both have been in therapy, and Joanne was admitted to attending EST sessions in an attempt to stop 'choosing to be in Paul's shadow' and to stop feeling guilty and inadequate about being what she refers to as 'a creative dilettante'.

When they are apart, Paul calls his wife several times a day, and according to more than one reporter he will break off in mid-sentence to say, 'I want to see my lady.'

Paul's remark in *Playboy* concerning staying faithful has become a classic: 'I have steak at home – why go out for hamburger?' Reportedly, Joanne was not amused by the remark, saying she didn't like being referred to as 'Paul Newman's meat.'

When reminded of this, Paul came up with a new metaphor. 'She's like a classy '62 Bordeaux,' he said of his wife. 'No, make it '59. That's a year that ages well in the bottle. Will I get in trouble for that?' he asked his interviewer impishly.

The fact is, Paul Newman adores his wife, and he's still in awe of her acting talent after all these years. 'I remember seeing her in Noel Coward's *Hay Fever*,' he said, referring to a play she was in years after their marriage, 'I thought, "I don't know that woman. She must be a real scorcher".'

Newman also enjoys referring to his wife as 'a voluptuary' in front of interviewers, making her blush. And he makes a concerted effort to keep the romance in their marriage alive and well. Once when Paul was on location in Hawaii (Joanne was there too) he handed her a box containing a new evening dress which he had picked out for her personally. After she had changed into the gown and he into evening clothes, they were transported to a local golf course where Paul had arranged for an elegant and intimate dinner to be served to them. The table was set beside the ocean, and they dined to the accompaniment of a string quartet.

'We're equals,' Paul says of his wife, 'but sometimes I'll forget how incredible she is, and then I'll see something that reminds me, like this room,' Paul told an interviewer, pointing to the elegant but comfortably furnished living room in their New York apartment. 'If anyone had ever told me twenty years ago that I'd be sitting in a room with peach walls, I'd have told them to take a nap in a urinal,' Newman (who has a taste for earthy language) remarked.

Joanne is just as crazy about her husband, but being an even more private person, she doesn't talk about it very much. One time, however, Woodward did say, 'I believe in advice my grandmother once gave me, and that is: 'When you pick a husband, remember that you have to be able to talk to him across the breakfast table for fifty years.'

Joanne not only remembered her grandmother's advice – she has also abided by it. After thirty years, she and Paul are still talking to each other over the breakfast table, and from all indications they will continue to do so. As Joanne said proudly, 'It's my first and only marriage.'

Chapter 10

1980 was the start of a new decade, which is always symbolic of new beginnings. In Paul Newman's life the timing couldn't have been better, because 1980 was literally the start of a fresh and vital new phase of his career.

In the spring of 1980, Paul began work on a new film, *Fort Apache, The Bronx*. Shot on location in New York City, the movie is about a police precinct in one of New York's toughest neighbourhoods, the South Bronx. In it, Newman plays a tough but compassionate cop named Murphy. A 17-year veteran of the force, Murphy has a special feeling of compassion for the black and Hispanic community he serves and a special understanding of the problems they must contend with.

Paul says he was drawn to the role because the character of Murphy was more flamboyant and interesting than any that he'd played for a while. Murphy is a special kind of cop, a 'character' who often disarms (in more ways than one) his adversaries with his good humour and his generosity of spirit. The cold, unemotional distance which Haskell and others accused Newman of in his depiction of Harper in *The Drowning Pool* is gone here. Newman as Murphy is alive and responsive, both as a cop and as a man in his mid-fifties who is ready to take another chance on love. Sadly, his Hispanic girl friend, though college educated and a professional, has a heroin problem and ends up overdosing. One who is aware of events in Newman's personal life can't help wondering whether Murphy's moving response to this tragedy on screen had its roots in the very real death of his son only two years before.

At any rate, the film was a popular success, and Paul received excellent reviews for his performance. Instead of being able to bask in the feeling of well-being brought about by his first really successful picture in years, however, Newman had to suffer the ignominy – along with all the others involved in the film – of being accused of racism. The residents of the real South Bronx felt that the film portrayed them negatively, using sterotypes of blacks and Hispanics as drug users and criminals, and that none were given positive, upbeat roles.

'I don't like being called a racist pig and being told I give up my humanity for money,' Newman said. These were indeed ironic accusations against a man who over the years had worked for and donated large amounts of money to civil rights causes.

Paul was especially bitter about being personally attacked by some New York papers, which he claimed had misrepresented events that had taken place during the location shooting of *Fort Apache, The Bronx.*

'I was savaged by some papers after (the movie),' said Newman. 'I was most offended by the *New York Post.* But journalists and newspapers protect each other like doctors do,' he went on. 'They won't name the paper that did these things. They'll only say, "Mr Newman has attacked a New York newspaper."

'That's too bad, because if some papers are not accurate in their news stories, and report events that didn't occur, it damages the credibility of all papers, through guilt by association,' Paul said passionately. 'It's unfortunate when responsible newspapers won't take the irresponsible ones to task. So, I felt I'd like to do a picture about media abuse.'

Paul was referring to his next film, *Absence of Malice,* which concerns the responsibility of the press. Directed by the esteemed Sydney Pollack, with a screen-play written by an editor of the *Detroit Free Press*, the film couldn't have come along at a better time for Newman after his experience with the press after *Fort Apache, The Bronx*.

In it, Newman plays the role of Michael Gallagher, who is the innocent victim of a purposely inaccurate news story planted by the police. Sally Field plays a hot-shot reporter who was duped into writing the false story. Gallagher starts out as a hard-nosed businessman who gets in this whole mess for the simple reason that his father happened to have been a bootlegger. In the course of investigating another, complicated case, the police plant the false story, hoping it will get Gallagher angry enough to give any information he has about the past and his father.

Even above and beyond the press angle, Newman liked the film and the role of Gallagher. 'The character moves inside the plot,' he said. 'The film is propelled more by the story than by the character development alone, but the characters are important too. And that's okay. You can do some very interesting acting under those conditions,' Paul said.

The critics agreed, for while some of them found the plot convoluted and hard to follow, they had good things to say about Newman. Director Sydney Pollack, who had known Paul for over 30 years, was extremely impressed by Paul's work in *Absence of Malice*.

'There's a stillness in his acting now that is quite magnetic,' Pollack said. 'You feel his intelligence, you can see him thinking. He has the depth of a clear pool of water, not rippling or churning or tumbling.'

Sally Field, who played Newman's love interest, can also attest to his 'stillness' as an actor – as well as his politeness. It seems that Paul had a difficult time during a scene where he was supposed to knock Field down, ripping her blouse in the process. 'He kept trying to fake it,' Sally said of her courteous co-star.

Then again, Newman's reluctance to express violence may have had to do with the way he had decided to play the role of Gallagher. 'He knew a lot,' Paul said of his *Absence of Malice* character, 'and people who know a lot don't do very much with their bodies.'

Newman's acting style had become more spare and effortless. He stopped looking for his inspiration outside and began to look inside himself. After all these years, he had finally developed enough confidence to fully use the technique of 'Method' acting. For the fifth time he was nominated for a best actor Oscar for his work in *Absence of Malice*, but he had ceased to worry about Hollywood's assessments of his talent a long time ago. When he lost for the fifth time, he just shrugged, took it in his stride, and went on to his next film, *The Verdict*.

In it, Newman plays the role of Frank Galvin, a down-and-out Boston lawyer who has had five cases in three years. Now in his fifties, Galvin had had a bright future in his younger days. But, having been rail-roaded out of his law firm by a crooked senior partner, Galvin had turned to self-pity and heavy drinking. As the film starts, he is presented with his first challenging case in years. However, it is so challenging that it seems hopeless, since he would be representing the sister of a young woman who lies in a coma after being given the wrong anaesthetic by prominent doctors at a powerful Catholic hospital.

The lawyer representing the hospital's interest is played by James Mason, who makes his character menacing, cut-throat and compelling. He offers Galvin and his client $200,000 to settle, but against the advice of almost everyone, Galvin refuses the money in favour of a court battle. Meanwhile, though his odds of winning against the influential Catholic church and the establishment lawyers seem staggering, Galvin finds a new lease on life and a new confidence in himself and his future in law. Also memorable as both characters and actors are Jack Warden as Galvin's legal mentor, and Charlotte Rampling as his boozy, world-weary girlfriend.

Paul Newman's performance in *The Verdict* is nothing short of a tour de force. If there was any film in his career for which he deserved the best actor Oscar, this was it. But as usual, Newman was nominated and lost. This time the loss truly meant nothing to Newman – because finally, after all these years, he realised that he was a good, perhaps even great, actor.

'I'm just now beginning to learn something about acting,' Newman said shortly after completing *The Verdict*. 'I don't say that as a joke and I don't say it because I'm being modest,' he said, 'I don't think I ever had an immediate, spontaneous gift to do anything right.'

Further ruminating on his progress as any actor, Paul said, 'When I look at my old movies, I get gloomy because I can see myself consciously working to create the character,' he explained. 'In the scene in *Hud* when I was talking to my nephew and I said, "My Mamma loved me but she died," I was working too hard to find the emotions. I compare that to the scene at the end of *The Verdict*. The emotions were there, but you couldn't see the machinery,' Paul stated, finally giving himself the credit he deserved.

As it happened, Newman wasn't director Sidney Lumet's first choice to play Galvin. Robert Redford was actually cast in the role, but after trying to have the character of Galvin made less seamy, Redford dropped out – and his pal Paul jumped at the chance to play Frank Galvin, a character he could readily identify with.

Like many people, Lumet was greatly impressed by the excellence of acting which Newman displayed in *The Verdict*. 'Paul has always been one of the best actors we've got,' he said after the fact, 'but there was that great stone face and those gorgeous blue eyes and a lot of people assumed he couldn't act. He (Paul) got relegated to leading man parts and he wasn't using a quarter of his talent,' Lumet went on. 'Now he's able to cut loose and do sensational work.'

Redford, Newman's pal for years, agreed. He was probably talking about himself as well as Paul when he said, 'If you are tagged as a sex symbol, it stands to reason you're not a good actor. It's as though you can't have too many things or people get angry.'

While Newman's film career was enjoying a renaissance, Joanne found herself, through a fortunate sequence of events, about to open in an off-Broadway show in the fall of 1981. She was 51 (but looked considerably younger) and hadn't been on the New York stage for 17 years. The play *Candida*, by George Bernard Shaw was first produced in 1894 and certainly wasn't everyone's cup of tea. But Joanne was hoping it would appeal to enough serious theatre-goers to stay open for the full run and make some money – this time for the Circle in the Square Theatre in Greenwich Village, a nonprofit operation which was one of Joanne's current causes.

The play concerns Candida, a worthy wife who is married to the Rev. James Mavor Morell. 'Her husband adores her,' Joanne explained, 'but he has always been the more glamorous one in the public eye. It's a situation I could identify with,' she added. The plot thickens when a 19-year-old poet named Marchbanks falls madly in love with Candida. Eventually the two men ask Candida to choose between them and she reads the riot act, lecturing both of them on how incredibly selfish they are. Joanne sees the play as making a feminist statement and said, 'In this as in so many things, Shaw was ahead of his time. I think he thought women were at least equal to if not superior to men.'

Joanne explained that the project came about when Kenyon College (from which Paul graduated) opened a professional theatre on campus and asked Paul to direct a new play by Michael Cristofer there. He had written the play *The Shadow Box*, which Newman had directed for TV a few years earlier. 'I was already on the board of directors for the school,'

Joanne explained, 'so when I went out to see Paul's play, I saw a young actor in it named Tait Ruppert who was so marvellous that I said, 'Now I can do *Candida* – because I've found my Marchbanks.' So we tried it out there as a fund-raiser in May. We all liked it and I loved playing it and I'm also on the board of the Circle in the Square, so we worked it out. Michael Cristofer is directing it, and although all of us are pros, we don't want to think of this project as a Broadway gamble,' Joanne said. 'I don't want to tackle Broadway, and I don't want a long run.'

Joanne didn't have to worry about the success of the play. It was so well received that its run was extended through January 3rd, when it was originally slated to close on November 22nd.

Candida was only one of the projects Joanne was juggling at that time. In fact, she had discovered a whole new dimension of her creative talents by trying her hand at directing. She directed a film version of Shirley Jackson's last work, *Come Along With Me*, and a movie called *The Lover* for the American Film Institute.

'I love directing,' Joanne told an interviewer around the time that *Candida* opened. 'Directing has broadened my vision. I used to be narrowly concentrated on my own role. Now, when I act, I'm aware of everything that's happening around me.'

'My youngest child has left for boarding school,' Woodward also remarked around this same time. 'I have no kids at home for the first time in twenty-something years. I'm going back to acting class. I want to do more plays.' Full to bursting with creative plans and ideas, Joanne smiled and said, 'Before the age of 45, my life was a disaster. I'm the only person I know who enjoys growing old.'

Joanne wasn't the only person in her family who was buzzing with new ideas at this time. Suddenly, in 1982, during a lull in his film career, Paul Newman decided to go into the food business, of all things, bottling salad dressing under the Newman's Own label. Paul had always had a 'thing' about salad dressing. He always made his own, with an oil and vinegar base, and he was sure it was the world's best.

As a consequence he is very fussy about salad dressings in restaurants and always insists on making his own. Joanne remembers being embarrassed by this obsession of her husband's, especially when she first became aware of it during the early days of their marriage.

One time they were in Chasen's, a posh restaurant in Los Angeles. 'It was one of our first stylish meals out,' Joanne recalls, 'and he took an already oiled salad to the men's room, washed it clean, dried it with towels, and returned to the table to do things right, with oil cut by a dash of water.'

Newman's homemade salad dressing proved very popular with friends, and at Christmas Paul took to making up bottles of it and giving it as gifts. Early in 1982, he decided to try making a business out of it, along with his friend and neighbour in Westport, author A.E. Hotchner, an authority on the life and works of Hemingway.

'I couldn't think of anything tackier than putting my name and reputation on a bottle of salad dressing, so I did it,' Newman said with his characteristic irreverence. 'No one expected it to be successful.'

But it was – so much so that Newman and his partner expanded their business first to include Newman's Own Oldstyle Picture Show Popcorn and then his Industrial Strength Venetian Marinara Spaghetti Sauce. All of the products released under the Newman's Own label are really favourites of his. Ever since the early 1960s, for instance, Newman was known for carrying around bags of his own personally popped popcorn, lightly salted and buttered, handshaken, and mysteriously, almost greaseless. Newman not only made this snack for his own consumption, but would also give it out at private screenings or movie outings with his friends.

Before the Newmans were married, one of their favourite

New York pastimes was to sit in the last row of the balcony at Radio City Music Hall, crunching on Paul's popcorn. As soon as the noise of the film allowed, Paul would pop open two of the four cans of beer which Joanne would smuggle into the theatre in her handbag.

Paul especially enjoys writing the wacky sayings that decorate the labels on his products, and he greatly enjoys overseeing the business. But there is a serious side to the Newman's Own products because, with the generosity and greatness of spirit he has always shown, Newman, along with his partner Hotchner, who serves as vice president and treasurer of the company, donates virtually all of the profits to charities and worthy causes. In a typical year, the company allocated money to the Scott Newman Center in California; a relief effort for Ethiopian famine victims; the Actors Studio, the Cystic Fibrosis Foundation; a maritime museum; a college science laboratory; historical societies; cancer and AIDS research; and *The New York Times* Neediest Cases Fund.

Just recently Newman's Own came out with two new products – microwave popcorn in two flavours, and lemonade. The lemonade was Joanne's idea and it is based on a recipe handed down in her family. Given a suitably whimsical title by Paul, Newman's Own Old Fashioned Roadside Virgin Lemonade, the commercial variety is made from water, fructose, lemon juice, lemon oil and lemon pulp and is sold in half gallon containers.

Newman and his partner hope the new products are as successful as the old ones, especially since they have a whole new project to fund – a camp for children who are afflicted with leukaemia and other life-threatening forms of cancer. Newman and Hotchner donated $4 million in profits from their company (all the government will allow) and made up the other $4 million that was needed to build and endow the camp by donations from other businesses and charities. Philanthropist Armand Hammer donated money made from selling paintings by Monet, Renoir and other artists from his gallery. In the autumn of 1987 it was announced that King Fahd and the people of Saudi Arabia had donated $5 million to the camp.

Located in a wooded area of north-eastern Connecticut, the summer retreat for sick children is called 'The Hole in the Wall Camp' after the gang of outlaws in *Butch Cassidy and the Sundance Kid*. It has a simulated Western village, with log cabins, corrals, a music hall, and even a 'saloon' with swinging doors.

The camp, planned with the help of doctors from the prestigious Yale-New Haven Medical Center, is partly staffed by cancer specialists from the institution and will be medically equipped for the needs of the campers, who can attend free of charge.

'The primary mission of the camp is to serve children with catastrophic blood diseases from the ages of 7 to 17,' said Dr. Howard Pearson, head of paediatric services at Yale-New Haven. 'We want to give them a memorable experience. For many, it will be their only time away from home except a visit to the hospital.'

So, for Paul Newman fans, a trip to the supermarket to buy Newman's Own – brands of salad dressing, spaghetti sauce, popping corn or lemonade – is the best thing audiences could do for Paul, aside from going to see his films.

In June of 1983, Newman found himself on location in Fort Lauderdale, Florida, filming *Harry and Son*. Not only was he starring in it; he was also director and co-producer. He had even collaborated with Ronald L. Buck on the script which was loosely adapted from a novel, *A Lost King* by Ray de Capite. Down under the Florida sun, Newman was sweating under the pressures of 'wearing so many hats' at the same time for the same film. 'It's just too tough,' he said. 'After a 12-hour day you go back and see an hour of film, and then you sit down and try to rewrite.'

During his ordeal, Paul was comforted by the presence of

not only his wife Joanne who co-starred in the film, but by his three daughters as well. Almost grown up at that point, they clowned around with their father during his few hours of freedom. Nell, 24, referred to him affectionately as 'old skinny legs'.

Harry and Son is a deeply personal and moving film about family relationships. The tension of the plot is generated by the conflict between Harry (Newman) who loses his job as a crane operator because of failing eyesight, and his son Howard (Robby Benson) who wants to be a writer.

'If this isn't Howard's picture, then somewhere along the line I've made a terrible mistake,' Newman said. 'The movie is strange in that it doesn't have the normal kind of plot thrust ... I suppose it's something like an impressionistic painting. We just kind of flung some characters up on the canvas and hoped they would stick,' he said, laughing.

The film rang true emotionally and received decent reviews. One of its most moving scenes was the one in which Howard comes running along the beach and up onto the back deck of the house – only to find his father lying dead on the floor inside. The son lifts up his father and lays his inert body on the bed.

Newman asked his wife to direct this scene. It took several takes, and after the first one, Joanne, in tears, rushed over to Paul, who got up and put his arms around her. In a very tender moment, Joanne hugged her husband and said, 'Oh, Paul, I'm so glad you didn't die.'

Joanne cried after each of the takes, and after the final one, Paul Newman hugged his wife and gave her a passionate, loving kiss.

As soon as *Harry and Son* was finished, Paul took off on the racing circuit. While editing the film, he planned to race four days a week. On the subject of combining acting and racing, Paul passed along something his wife had said: 'Joanne has an interesting theory that I was really getting bored as an actor, which is why I started racing,' Newman explained, 'and that some of the passion for that has bled back into acting. I don't know if that's true, but it's an interesting theory.'

Newman wasn't nominated for an Oscar in *Harry and Son* but in 1986, he finally did receive an Academy Award. It wasn't for any film, but one of those 'honorary Oscars' which Hollywood usually hands out to actors and actresses who are in their advanced old age.

According to Newman's friend and lawyer, Irving Axelrad, Newman was going to refuse this 'honour'. 'He said they'd always treated him as second,' Axelrad said, 'and now they were acting as if he was old and through.'

But with his usual good grace, Newman accepted the Oscar. Little did he dream that in just a year's time he would finally receive the best actor Oscar that had been denied him for so many years.

Chapter 11

Newman had been 36 when he played Fast Eddie Felson in *The Hustler*. Almost incredibly, in 1986 at the age of 61, Newman was asked to revive his role as the pool player who had allowed his talent to be misused.

It was famed director Martin Scorsese who got interested in this project. He, in turn, got Touchstone-Disney and Newman interested.

'I didn't want to be involved in a literal sequel, in which you had to know what the first film was about in order to understand the second,' Scorsese explained. What really interested him was the character of Fast Eddie Felson and where that character would be 25 years after *The Hustler* ended.

Scorsese discovered that several treatments for a *Hustler* sequel had been attempted over the years. The author, Walter Revis, since deceased, had even written a sequel to his original novel, but Scorsese wasn't too thrilled with it.

Scorsese hired novelist Richard Price, author of *The Wanderers*, a fellow New Yorker who had a fine eye and ear for people from the seamier side of life and who could depict them in a strikingly realistic way. Scorsese's next move was to bring Price and 'Fast Eddie' together. This meeting took place in a beach house on the California coast which Newman had rented in order to get some much-needed rest and relaxation.

165

Scorsese, who had first seen Newman on the big screen when he was 12, was nervous at the prospect of meeting a legend face to face. The reality of this meeting was even more jarring than he had imagined. A lot of it had to do with 'culture shock'.

'We're sitting there on the porch, and it was too bright,' Scorsese explained. 'I've got on a blue blazer, jeans, sunglasses. Richard (Price) is all hunched over. Y'know we're these two New York scuzzballs. And Newman's out in the sun in a bathing suit and he says, "Come on out." And he's saying things like, "You know, this morning I got in the shower and I ate an Israeli melon." And Richard is looking at me as if to say, "What is he talking about?" I don't know what he is talking about either,' Scorsese maintained. 'Doesn't he realise he's talking to two New York lower East side-type guys . . . Israeli melons? He's talking about a sensuality we don't understand.'

But when the three sat down to work, they discovered that they were all pretty much in accord as far as the *Hustler* spin off was concerned. Once the three were able to decide on characters and work out the general plot, Price came up with a screenplay which was well-received by most critics.

'The new film delves a great deal into internal conflicts – internal dramas, manipulations, control,' Scorsese said. 'It's about the changing of values. And it's a much more introspective picture. Eddie – he's lost it, he's lost the will to play pool – we never know why. But he's become a sharp character nevertheless. He's become a stakehorse – a man who has a stable of young pool players whom he sponsors.

'He sees this young kid who's just a wonderful pool player,' Scorsese went on, 'but the kid doesn't understand anything about money, or anything about cheating to make even more money. So Eddie takes the kid under his wing and starts to corrupt him. But of course things don't exactly go the way he plans – especially his own feelings. Taking the kid on the road, he's really facing himself. Instead of the education of the kid, it's *his* education.'

Besides Tom Cruise as Vincent Lauria and Newman as Eddie, the cast of *The Color of Money* included Mary Elizabeth Mastrantonio as Carmen, Vincent's streetwise girlfriend, and Helen Shaver as Eddie's love interest.

'There was a feeling of camaraderie about this film that was very special,' Newman said. 'There was a sense of selflessness on the part of all the people connected with it; an enthusiasm to try new things.'

During the filming a special bond between Paul Newman and Tom Cruise evolved. Between takes, they, lark around, playing pool or going for rides in Cruise's new Porsche. But their favourite pastime was trying to out-do each other with really bad jokes.

'Tom really felt like he was in pig heaven,' said producer Irving Azelrad. 'They had a wonderful relationship, more like brothers than "Gramps" and "the kid".' (Two of their pet names for each other.)

Newman and Cruise were a winning combination in terms of the film also. Teenagers and young adults who had been impressed by Cruise in *Top Gun* were anxious to see him again on screen, while Paul Newman's many fans (plus film buffs who had loved the original *Hustler*) were anxious to see how 'Fast Eddie' had fared over the years.

For the most part, *The Color of Money*, and Paul Newman, received rave reviews. According to Peter Travers in *People* magazine, 'Paul Newman makes everything he's learned in three decades of screen acting pay off in this forceful follow-up to his 1961 role as pool shark Fast Eddie Felson in *The Hustler*. But don't expect one of those ravaged, old pro performances. At 61, Newman hasn't lost his looks; he's improved upon them. And his acting isn't lazy; it's eager, feral. He's in full maturity, and he's never been better.'

Vincent Canby in *The New York Times* said: 'Mr. Newman appears to be having a ball as the ageing but ever-resilient Fast Eddie. It's a wonderfully funny, canny performance, set off by the actor's intelligence that shines through the character without upstaging it.'

As we all know by now, Paul Newman finally did win the Best Actor of 1986 Academy Award for his role in *The Color of Money*. While everyone who loved Paul as a person and admired him as an actor was happy for him, many felt that the award had been too late in coming to have any real meaning. Surely no one blamed Newman for not being present at the ceremony to receive it.

By the time *The Color of Money* premiered, Paul and Joanne were busy working on a film project together – making a movie of one of their favourite Tennessee Williams's plays, *The Glass Menagerie*. Paul directed the film, with an excellent cast headed up by Joanne Woodward and including Karen Allen, John Malkovich and James Naughton. The finished film was praised for its richness of characterisation and range of emotion. While largely ignored in America, *The Glass Menagerie* was honoured by showings at both the Cannes and the Toronto Film Festivals in 1987.

What else is new with Paul and Joanne? Well, he's still racing his Nissan GTO 33ZX Turbo around every fast track he can find. Between April and October 1987, Newman competed in no less than five International Motor Sports Association GTO Races. In addition, he is involved in his Newman's Own business, and of course the Hole in The Wall Camp, which is nearing completion.

As for Joanne, she's busy both with acting and directing, in projects which she feels are worthwhile. For instance, she starred in the sensitive and timely TV special entitled *Do You Remember Love?* about a woman suffering from Alzheimer's disease. Joanne was very gratified to learn that the TV special resulted in increased contributions to agencies formed to help people deal with this tragic affliction.

Joanne also found time in 1987 to direct Shirley Knight in the play *The Depot*, about an ordinary housewife who becomes involved in the nuclear disarmament movement.

Joanne, who feels very strongly about this subject, is working to put together a television adaptation of this powerful and important play.

What's ahead for Paul Newman and Joanne Woodward? Judging from their past, anything is possible. Surely this talented and multi-faceted pair will find many more challenging and creative things to do, both together and separately. As Shakespeare put it in one of his sonnets, theirs is 'a marriage of true minds', and this will continue to be so even as their careers and talents diverge into new directions, bringing them even more fulfilment as time goes on.

★ ★ ★ ★ ★